TEXAS COUNTRY REPORTER

TEXAS COUNTRY REPORTER

Stories from the Backroads

Bob Phillips

The
Globe
Pequot
Press

GUILFORD, CONNECTICUT

Cover design by Libby Kingsbury
Cover photos by Phillips Productions, Inc.; flag image © PhotoDisc, Inc.
Text design by Nancy Freeborn/Freeborn Design
Photo credits: p. 83 © Index Stock Imagery; all others by Phillips Productions, Inc.

Library of Congress Cataloging-in-Publication Data

Phillips, Bob, 1951–
    Texas country reporter : stories from the backroads / Bob Phillips.
          p. cm.
    ISBN 0–7627–0715–1 (hardcover) — ISBN 0–7627–0714–3 (pbk.)
    1. Texas—Description and travel—Anecdotes. 2. Texas—Social life and customs—20th century—Anecdotes. 3. Texas—Biography—Anecdotes.
4. Country life—Texas—Anecdotes. I. Title.

F391.2 .P47 2000
976.4—dc21

                                                00–034108

First Edition/First Printing
Printed in Canada

TO MY HERO AND MENTOR, THE LATE CHARLES KURALT,

WHO PIONEERED THE IDEA OF TRAVELING THE BACKROADS.

CONTENTS

Passionate People

The Good Old Ways

Artists of All Kinds

Lone Star Legacy

Creatures Great & Small

Roadside Texas

ACKNOWLEDGMENTS

There are countless individuals who have made this book possible, including all the folks I like to refer to simply as "the salt of the earth," who graciously shared their stories with me so I could share them with you.

This book was the brainchild of my editor, Laura Strom. She and her staff really did the work. All I had to do was tell them what I know.

In the almost 30 years that I've been traveling the backroads, I have had many good traveling companions. Some of them helped with this book, including Jason Anderson and Brian Hawkins, who not only offered great assistance with the writing, but also were responsible for the really good photographs. The mediocre pictures were my own. Christy Carnes, Martin Perry, Brenda Carver, Sharon Varnell, Gene Bryant, Brooke Maples, Clay Marshall, and Brandon Bloodworth were very helpful in pulling together all the elements necessary to turn television stories into stories for this book.

In doing that, we have attempted to print the stories as they were at the time when they first aired on our television show. Some of the details have changed since then; some of the people mentioned here are no longer with us. Their stories, however, still tell an important tale.

INTRODUCTION

I was a real journalist once. One of those guys who wrote and reported news stories about fires, wrecks, city council meetings, and school board elections. I even spent time as a news and sports photographer, traveling for several years with the Dallas Cowboys and shooting on the sidelines for NFL Films. It was exciting, but my heart wasn't in it.

The stories that interested me were the ones about people you've never heard of before, the tales of ordinary folks doing extraordinary things, of regular men and women going about their lives. I always liked the positive, feel good kind of stories that make you smile or bring a lump to your throat. Those were the ones I wanted to tell.

In 1972 some other news guys and I, all employees of a Dallas television station, decided to try to do just that—tell those stories in a weekly program. If people liked it, we said, we'd continue. If they didn't, we'd go back to the fires and wrecks. Almost thirty years later, I'm still telling those stories every week. The only difference is that I left that television station so that I could syndicate my show and tell my stories to a lot more people. But the stories, and the people they are about, are still the same.

For a reason we can't explain, the change of the centuries made us feel that perhaps we should try to recall some of our favorites from all those years. What follows are fifty of those stories. They're illustrated with photos we took along the way and with images pulled straight from the television programs. Wherever possible we've provided updates on how our friends are doing and where they are now. These stories represent only a small portion of our favorites, but we hope they'll give you an idea of what we do and why we do it.

Our program is a celebration of life. We hope you will read this book and celebrate with us.

BAT MAN FROM ROBINSON

Robinson

e meet lots of folks who have two lives. They're not hiding anything, it's just that there's the life they live to feed their families and then there's the life they live to feed their souls. It's that second life we're always looking for. Tell me about a guy who goes to work at Wal-Mart every day from eight to five and I'll ask you, "What's the story?" But tell me about a guy who can't wait to get home to make, build, or create something—who lives for that other life—and I'm already in the car on my way to see what this guy is about.

Over the years, peddling prescriptions has treated Rob Sellers well. In fact, he's quite a hit at the pharmacy. But deep down, he always had a creative urge. And one day he decided to do something about it.

Rob: *I'm the pharmacy manager of Wal-Mart. I've been working for Wal-Mart for twelve years now. That's where I make a living. I enjoy helping people, that's what I do. But there are times when you need a break from doing what you do for a living.*

So after a decade of delays, Rob decided to step up to the plate.

Rob: *I started making bats. I just decided, hey—let's combine my love of sports and a love for woodworking and see if I can make something out of it. We live in Robinson, and I've been known as the Bat Man here for a while. I am Bat Man in Robinson.*

With names like Louisville and Easton as competition, Rob knew he'd never be a contender, so he decided to make his own market. These aren't just your ordinary run-of-the-mill baseball bats— they are custom-made, one-of-a-kind trophy bats. Now Rob's got his hands full.

Rob: *It takes me about four days to make a bat from start to finish. I can put any kind of logo, any name, anything on there to personalize it. It's hard work. It's not easy to do, and I enjoy doing it, but it is a whole lot of hard work.*

Hours of sweat and sawdust can't slow Rob Sellers down—in fact, that's what helps keep him going. It's the satisfaction of a hard day's work. But it's more than that. It's knowing that every day he's turning out handmade wooden reminders of a simpler way of life.

> **Rob:** *I like the tradition of a wooden baseball bat. It really does take you back to your childhood when you got that first wooden baseball bat that you enjoyed playing with. I'm passing that onto my kids and their friends, so it's been a lot of fun for me.*

After all is said and done, it isn't really making bats that makes Rob's day. It's spending time with his kids and getting to share with them just a little bit of his childhood. He says his bats help bring them together, and for Rob Sellers, that makes every day a home run.

"THERE ARE TIMES WHEN YOU NEED A BREAK FROM DOING WHAT YOU DO FOR A LIVING."

> **Rob:** *You know, making bats is a lot of fun, but the most fun that I have is coming out here with the kids and playing with them. That's what brings me the most joy in doing this—that, and being able to work with my hands. It's something I can pass down from generation to generation. That's what makes it all worthwhile to me.*

TOWN WATCHMAN

Devine

I t's always good to spend some time in a town where the major concerns of the day are when and how much it's gonna rain, the Friday night football score, and what kind of price cattle are bringing down at the auction barn. For certain, one thing they don't worry about in Devine, Texas, is crime, because Eddie Hutsler is on patrol.

Eddie Hutsler is, without a doubt, the nosiest man in town. And people here wouldn't have it any other way.

Policeman: *There's not anybody in town that doesn't know Eddie. Eddie's kind of a night watchman. You know, he goes around, he checks every business that's in town—checks to make sure that the door's locked. He's prevented several burglaries around town just by him calling us in.*

Nobody knows exactly how long Eddie's been checking doors in Devine. But not once has he ever missed his nightly ritual of tugging, twisting, and turning every doorknob, latch, and lock for miles around. Eddie is an uncomplicated and quiet man who has formed a rare partnership with everyone here. At night, Eddie takes care of the town, and in the daytime, the town takes care of Eddie. The Devine city council chambers are home, and Eddie's taken up residence in an out-of-the-way corner.

Policeman: *We got him the cot for this past Christmas, but he prefers just to sleep in that old chair that he sits in. We asked him why he doesn't use the cot. He said he's just so used to sleeping in the chair, where, as I understand it, he's probably slept for the last ten years or more. When he's done for the evening checking the doors, he'll come in, watch a little TV, and he'll go to sleep, get up, and do it again.*

Townsperson 1: *He knows everyone. Knows everything about everyone. If Eddie doesn't come in in the mornings and we don't see him at lunch, we start looking for him. We get worried about him.*

Townsperson 2: *We don't have much of a problem because Eddie's always around. He keeps an eye on our town. We all love Eddie.*

Townsperson 3: *He has diabetes now. So the doctor has him on a special diet. He'll come in to eat lunch, and he'll say, "Well, can I eat this, can I eat that?" We kind of watch him on his food.*

Townsperson 4: *I've been employed with Dairy Queen for over twelve years now. And in that length of time, I don't think there's a day that's gone by that he hasn't come in and sat down and had a cup of coffee. He comes around, and he always makes a point of saying, "I checked your doors last night."*

AT NIGHT, EDDIE TAKES CARE OF THE TOWN, AND IN THE DAYTIME, THE TOWN TAKES CARE OF EDDIE.

Townsperson 3: *There's a lot of people out there that won't go out and work, but Eddie will.*

Eddie's one person in the world who doesn't know the meaning of the word charity. He works for every dime at a job with terrible hours and endless hazards.

Eddie: *I like to do this kind of work. I'm proud of this work. I ain't got nothing else to do. Gotta work to earn money. Nobody's gonna give it to you. I pick up beer cans, too.*

Eddie is a quiet, constant reassurance in this south Texas community. A man who's keeping up with the world by keeping an eye on the tiny town of Devine.

Townsperson 3: *It's going to be sad one of these days when Eddie's not around to take care of our town.*

MOM, APPLE PIE, AND CHEVROLET

Lubbock

or all practical purposes, Bill Clement owns a junkyard right on the outskirts of Lubbock, Texas. In Bill's yard you'll find hundreds of rusty, rotten reminders of automobiles past. The way we see it, if you call this a junkyard, then you'd call Bill a junk man. But what Bill Clement has here is the self-proclaimed largest collection of old Chevrolets in the known universe. That's why we call him the Chevy Man.

Bill: *This is a lifetime collection of old Chevrolets. I've been here at this location about sixteen years. So you're looking at the accumulated sixteen years of cars that didn't sell or cars that weren't good enough to sell that we used for parts instead.*

You'll probably never find anyone, anywhere, that knows more about old Chevys than Bill Clement. Over the years, he's owned 4,000 of them. Some he's sold, some he's kept, some he's used for parts. On the day we met Bill, he was collecting parts.

Bill: *There are a lot of parts on this car that look bad. Kind of like the old joke—they look bad but they feel good. They work. So, a little cleanup and a little paint, and a little time. And they're good as new again.*

According to Bill, nearly every one of these old junkers is suitable for restoration. But for a few, this is their last resting place after a long, hard life.

Bill: *Well, that one's dead. Somebody has attacked this poor old car and beat it with a hammer. Must have put a big block engine in it. Look at these mounts, the welding. That is unbelievable. This poor car has been brutally assaulted. It may never heal up. If you want to see another terrible cruelty to a vehicle, this one used to be a Nomad wagon. Somebody has made it into a pickup. And they have literally used wheelbarrows full of Bondo to create this monstrosity and, in doing that, they ruined a $5,000 car and turned it into dumpster bait. You want to see another sick item? They've cut this out with a tomahawk so they could put bigger tires on it. This is a neat old car. It's a Bel Air two-door sedan, a '55 and they didn't* *make a whole lot of 'em. It's a shame to have a car like this and to have this kind of treatment done to it. Because this would have made a real nice restoration, but it's dead meat. It's really just parts now. Every one of 'em speak. They all grieve about the cruelties, the inhuman punishment that they've received.*

If you ask Bill, Chevrolet stopped making cars in 1972. That was the last year for the gas-guzzling muscle cars. And Bill says it was also the last year for the American love affair with the automobile.

Bill: *Yea, I think a lot of these old cars. This was America at its zenith. People all over the world recognized America as the car people, and Chevrolet was the leading American car. It outsold every other manufacturer every year from 1927. It's Mom, apple pie, the flag, and Chevrolet. You keep 'em because they can give things to other cars to make them go again. You take a piece off of one, and you put it on one that doesn't run, and it goes again. So there's a lot of cannibalism going on here.*

Bob: *You make it sound like reincarnation.*

Bill: *That's why they call it re-in-car-nation. That's where the word came from, taking the nuts and bolts off of one of these old dead soldiers to put another one back on the street.*

Bill's latest restoration job is a '55 Chevy convertible. All 1955 parts, all Chevrolet, all American.

Bill: *A little surgery and a little money and a little time and—well, it won't ever be as good as new because nobody can beat the General's assembly back in those years. The General, the Chevrolet motor car company, was really a high quality organization during those years. These cars were built like a tank.*

Bill sometimes takes up to two years to turn a rusty old hulk into something that he'll tool down the highway in a couple of times and then let go to the highest bidder. All for a few memories of a time when gas was cheap and spirits were high. A time Bill Clement doesn't want to forget.

Bill: *I love it. I just can't be without a ragtop. When the weather's nice, I got to let the top down and let the little girl dance.*

Bob: *Do you get attached to these cars?*

Bill: *Not at all. They're just friends and acquaintances. I realize that I can't have them all, and I can't keep 'em all, so it's fun to know 'em and it's fun to have 'em and on to the next one. You know, after four thousand of 'em, you better not get attached.*

Far as Bill's concerned, you can't drive these beauties just anywhere, anyway.

> "THIS WAS AMERICA AT ITS ZENITH. . . . PEOPLE WERE A LITTLE PROUDER TO BE TEXANS AND A LITTLE PROUDER TO BE AMERICANS."

Bill: *Route 66 is about the only highway that I feel good going down in one of these cars. Between Amarillo and Oklahoma City, there are pieces of the old highway still there, and you really get a buzz like you've made a time trip back to the old days. Stop and get gas, and people just ooh and aah. They're having a big time. They're having as good a time as I am just looking at the old car and talking about how it used to be.*

Bob: *Did it used to be better?*

Bill: *Yea, it really did. I think it did. The people were a little prouder to be Texans and a little prouder to be Americans, and it was a different time, different era. We had some pretty good things going for us back then. The old music, the old roads, the old gas, the old way. It just feels right to be going down a narrow old road in an old car with the top down. Running seventy miles an hour, it's like it used to be. It feels like time's right again!*

SINCE OUR STORY . . .

In 1999 Bill Clement decided to give up the Chevy business, but not before completing one final restoration—that of singer Buddy Holly's 1958 Impala. After that Bill bought Lubbock radio station KDAV (KDAV is the radio station where Buddy Holly got his start). He is now a disk jockey at the station, which only plays "feel good" music from the 1950s. You can listen to KDAV-AM on the world wide web at KDAV.com.

TEST OF FIRE

Lubbock

D o you remember your first mud pie? Chances are you had no idea what you were doing. Still, the call of that strange mixture of water and earth was too strong to ignore. So you set out making something, anything. It really didn't matter what, just as long as you could get your hands into it and feel it take shape beneath your fingers. Well Eddie Dixon became a sculptor in much the same way most of us learned to make mud pies.

Eddie: *When I first started working, I started out with a stick and a butter knife. I was using wax that I was going to make a candle out of. I didn't know anything about it. And I didn't know anything about equipment either. It was kind of like a quest for fire.*

Eddie Dixon's quest for sculpture began back in college, back in the days when the world was wide and he had the talent and the smarts to do most anything. Today, talking to him, you get the feeling he did it all. He will tell you stories about walking point in Vietnam, and about Berkeley, where he earned advanced degrees in chemistry, zoology, and entomology. He will tell you about trading stocks in Chicago and about the days he was a member of the Black Panthers. But it's when talk turns to sculpting that you will get an unexpected peek into Eddie Dixon's soul.

Eddie: *Why I do what I do is because I find satisfaction in it. I enjoy creating beauty. I enjoy the hand-eye coordination or the thought process. And it absolutely amazes me how I do it. It's God-given. Become wealthy, and you live, you die, you've spent money. So what? What else have you done? What are you all about?*

What Eddie Dixon is about is capturing a moment, an emotion, or a personality and forever freezing in bronze the sorrow and the pain, the pride and the joy of his subjects. The sculptures tell a story, if you're willing to look deep enough and listen to the passion born from an artist's hands.

Eddie: *More important than anything else is if you can move somebody. If you can move somebody from apathy to sympathy, and if you can influence someone somewhere in their life when they see your work, then you'll feel it hasn't been done in vain.*

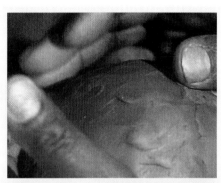

A finished piece of bronze is more than one man's handiwork. It is the collective sum of a half dozen dedicated craftsmen. Eddie provides the creative foundation. But it's the folks at House Bronze in Lubbock who breathe bronze life into Eddie's wax creations.

Eddie: *It never ceases to amaze me how you have a plain piece of bronze or polished metal and how it's heated, how the colors come out. When you have someone that's a master at his work, he's an artist. He's an artist because he can make or break the artist.*

For certain, Eddie's lifelike creations are not abstract. The story being told here is one of history and the people who lived it. And from enormous monuments to tabletop busts, his work has gained international attention.

Eddie: *It's almost like it takes on a life of its own. And you're not even conscious sometimes of what you're doing. But it's happening, you're living that time, you're living that era of history. You're empathetic with the individual, and you're striving to express what he's feeling. And you have to feel that almost yourself.*

At House Bronze, the casting is always an occasion. For Eddie, it's the moment in which his delicate creation stands the test of heat and fire. And it is within his white-hot sculpture and glowing molten metal that Eddie Dixon sees an analogy to life.

Eddie: *We all have to stand the test of fire. And if we can pass through that test of fire, then we'll be as refined as gold, and as beautiful as a well-done sculpture. That's the fire, that is what I see in the fire. I see how it burns, how it purifies. Maybe we should all go through a test of fire. I think we would have a much better world. A more refined world, a more refined nation.*

Eddie's quest for perfection has no end. Just when he thinks he's reached it, he finds it's gone.

Eddie: *I'm constantly being awed by the things that I accidentally do, and I say, "How do I do this over again?" And sometimes it's like a trumpeter playing a tune that isn't there, or you see this thing and you want to possess it too, but you only get a glimpse of it once, and then it's gone, it's transitory. That's what I see goodness or perfection as. You only get a glimpse of it every now and then, and when you do, it causes you to shudder. 'Cause it's almost frightening. I endeavor to create perfection.*

Eddie Dixon could have been a scientist or a stockbroker or even a professional soldier if things had turned out differently. You might have found Eddie doing any one of those things, and you probably would have never heard of him. We found Eddie Dixon tucked away in a makeshift studio at a foundry in Lubbock, Texas, doing what he feels has become his destiny.

Eddie: *My objective, or goal, is to leave a legacy for the generations coming. To tell the generations to follow that the light at the end of the tunnel is not another train coming. It's hope. If my work can move one person or change something in someone for the good, I think that I have accomplished a lot. If it's just one person, one person, then I've accomplished something.*

A TALL SHIP FOR TEXAS

Galveston

We meet lots of folks who do interesting things for a living. But sometimes it's the things people do *for free* that catch our attention. Especially when those volunteer hours require a lot of hard work. *Elissa*, a 111-year-old lady of the sea, is known as the tall ship for Texas—a tall ship manned entirely by a volunteer crew. She unfurls her sails to the wind only a few days each year.

It's a special morning at Pier 21 in Galveston, Texas. The *Elissa* is about to set sail in the waters of the Gulf of Mexico. After six months of training on weekends and after work, her crew is ready for the high seas.

Crew member 1: *It's my first time as a crew member. And these lines are tough when they get wet. I'm retired and I enjoy it. I'm looking for something new to do. An incredible amount of work goes in with the training. Lots of volunteer hours for a little bit of sailing.*

Crew member 2: *This is probably one of the only places in the country where the average person on the street can come and learn to sail a square-rigger. Usually you have to go into a maritime academy or something like that.*

From all walks of life, they have come together to work as a team, to learn the art of sailing and to discover the love for the sea. Johnny Towell is one of the people who saved this ship.

Johnny: *For myself, it's just a love. I feel like every time I come down here, I get more out of it than I give to the ship. I think of it a lot like I do a hobby. It's something to do on weekends. I don't play golf, I don't play tennis. I come down and work on Elissa.*

They started work on the *Elissa* in 1975. She was nothing more than a decrepit, rusting hulk of iron destined for the scrap heap. But people with a vision found her in a Greek shipyard. The folks at the Galveston Historical Foundation saw in the *Elissa* a new icon for their city and a prize for the state of Texas. Through hundreds of donations and thousands of hours of labor, craftspeople from across the country gathered in Galveston to make her again what she once was—a grand sailing ship from the turn of the century.

Johnny: *It's a love for the sea, a love for preservation. A lot of man-hours and a lot of money went into getting the Elissa sailworthy, ready for the seas again. Actually, a lot of people thought it never would sail again. But as you can see, it's doing it and doing it well.*

This is the seventh year of sailing for the new *Elissa*. In that time, this group of ragtag volunteers and Captain Jay Bolton have become the envy of the sailing world.

Jay: *It's recognized by the international tall ship community as being the finest restored tall ship in the world, and as such, she is truly a celebrity. When I took her to New York*

for the Statue of Liberty celebration, captain after captain would come over from his grand tall ship just to see the Elissa. So she is truly a unique ship. And to sail with volunteers of this caliber is really what is rare throughout the world. That has really been the ultimate in my satisfaction—watching these volunteer people become professional seamen and very expert at sailing a square-rigger. That's really neat.

We had to wonder why anyone would invest so much time in something that seems like so much hard work—pulling ropes, climbing masts, washing decks. We had to wonder what it is about this ship that draws so many people to her. So we asked, and Randy Morivan told us all we needed to know.

"IT'S A LOVE FOR THE SEA, A LOVE FOR PRESERVATION."

Randy: *The lady being as gentle as she is, you know, when she commands attention, she generally gets it. And it's amazing how most of the volunteers have the same feeling. It's emotion that not many of us can explain to you, but we know it exists. When the sails start turning pink and green and blue and orange, you know. And when you see the sunset and the sunrise, and when the stars settle down at the top of the mast, you know. That sort of thing is where the emotion comes from. I have a small heritage in my blood that says I must sail. And then when I got a chance to sail with the Elissa, I found my place in life. That's why I sail here.*

John Masefield wrote, "I must go down to the sea again, to the lonely sea and the sky / And all I ask is a tall ship and a star to steer her by." Go in spirit to the sea and sail with this crew of volunteers. Turn her sails into the wind and taste the ocean air. Share the adventure. Sail the *Elissa*.

Johnny: *It's the tall ship for Texas. It's for everybody. It's for all of Texas and for all of America.*

FAMILY OF FARMERS
Hooks

Highway 8 up in Bowie County will carry you to or take you away from half a dozen tiny farm towns in the northeast corner of Texas. Over the last quarter century or so, it's mostly been carrying people away. The answer to the old question "How you gonna keep 'em down on the farm?" would seem to be—you don't. But there is one place up near Hooks, Texas, where the family farm is hanging on.

Brent Ramage is thirty years old. His brother Bart is thirty-three. Together with their daddy, Jewel, they run the family farm—600 acres spreading back off the banks of the Red River. Back when the brothers were born, one in every three families lived on a farm. Today, it's one in fifty.

Bob: *Why is it that you're still in the farming business when a lot of people are getting out?*

Brent: *Well, that's a pretty easy question. We only do things or plant crops or harvest crops or sell crops that we can produce for less than what we can sell it for.*

Bob: *Yet you're plowing over some of your hay fields right now. Gonna replant something else. Why is that?*

Brent: *Well, we felt that the hay market kind of sagged this year. As a matter of fact, there's less horses and less cows in East Texas. We don't want to have a crop or a product that's obsolete so we're experimenting with some other crops.*

The Ramages do not run your conventional family farm. You will not find a thrasher or combine on the place. What you will find are fields full of pecans and pumpkins—crops without price supports, crops that count on customers who simply want the real thing for a delicious homemade pie. When Brent and Bart's mother couldn't find a decent blueberry in town, the brothers planted her a bush. Today, the blueberries cover twenty-three acres.

But money isn't exactly falling off the trees these days. Any farmer and most anybody else will tell you that. So what you do if you're a family like the Ramages is you take the big barn that was home only to owls and alley cats, kick them outside, and open the Ramage Country Store and sell those delicious pie fixins' right there on the home place. There are pecans and peanut brittle, blueberries in season, and in the fall, pumpkins. Lots and lots of pumpkins. So far, in spite of a tough economy, the Ramages, three families full, are making it.

Bob: *When you all are together, do you tend to talk business much?*

Cindy Ramage: *We talk business, but that's just part of it. We try to put in our fun. We do other things too, but it eventually comes around to—well, we could do this to the store. We get these great ideas just sitting around talking.*

Bob: *So talk of the grandkids turns to talk of farming.*

Cindy: *That's right. Eventually.*

Bob: *Is this pretty much a seven-day-a-week job?*

Brent: *It's eight-day. Things really get hectic when we're harvesting hay and harvesting blueberries and trying to run the store and trying to maintain our marriages and sanity all at the same time.*

Ginger Ramage: *It just depends on where your priorities are. I'm not saying that it's not difficult at times. There are many times when I miss going to the theater and being more involved in other outside social activities, such as the church—although we are quite involved. But there are many times when you have to sacrifice the things that you want for the benefit of the farm. Because, if you do not, then you will sacrifice your business.*

Bob: *Any way that you'd ever get out of this business?*

Brent: *Well, when you go into farming it's not like some of your other jobs. It requires a lot of commitment—in management, time, and educational requirements. We made the commitment, and there's no way, unless something drastic happens, that we'll ever leave the farm. Because this is it. I think our best crop is the kids that we have. A pair of sons in both of our families plus our other nieces and nephews. I think that's one of our better crops.*

"A HUNDRED YEARS FROM NOW, THE ONLY MARK ON THE LAND WILL BE HOW YOU'VE CARED FOR IT."

Bob: *It's beautiful out here.*

Brent: *It is. But beauty is not what keeps people on the farm. It's something ingrained. There's a bond that has developed. I was raised on a farm. People that live in the city just don't really understand it. You know, a hundred years from now, the only mark on the land will be how you've cared for it. But you still don't own the land.*

Bob: *And you like that?*

Brent: *Well, that's just one of nature's rules. You're temporarily caretakers of it. It's the land that's been here for millions of years, and we just are here a very short time. It's given to you to watch over, but you never really own the land.*

SINCE OUR STORY . . .

Ramage Farms is an ever-expanding family business. The brothers are now building a restaurant on Interstate 30 that will welcome visitors as they arrive in Texas from Arkansas. The restaurant will be hard to miss, as it will be beneath a 70-foot silo decorated with a Texas flag.

STONE SKIPPER

Driftwood

ormer oil field worker Jerry McGhee is a wanderer, a dreamer, a man who sees unequaled beauty in the form of stones that lie at the bottom of the crystal-clear Blanco River in the Texas Hill Country. Give him a smooth, round, river rock, and just watch what he can do. You see, Jerry is a professional stone skipper. And believe it or not, he heads an outfit called the North American Stone Skipping Association.

You can keep the precious gems, rare limestone fossils, and expensive minerals. Just leave enough stones for Jerry McGhee to skim across the water's surface.

Jerry: *It doesn't matter what shape it is. It can be any shape. It just needs to be uniformly flat, and you really can't tell that until you stop and pick 'em up. It can be rectangular to triangular to irregular. As long as they're uniformly thick and large.*

Jerry just could be responsible for more ripples across more bodies of water than any other human being. From his office, just a stone's throw from the Blanco River, Jerry's mounting a global campaign to teach others the art of stone skipping.

Jerry: *People have skipped stones on water since ancient times. There's an American word for skipping stones that not many people are aware of. It's called "dap." To dap is to skip stones in American. The British call it "ducks and drakes."*

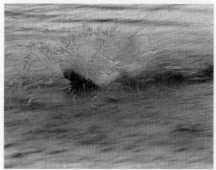

Skipping stones may not ever become the great American pastime, but membership in the association is growing. In fact, the Blanco River has played host to the world championship stone-skipping competition for the last several years, and Jerry is writing his second book on the art and science of stone skipping.

Jerry: *The Guinness world record is thirty-eight skips. And we did that on the Blanco River, off of Fisher Store Bridge.*

Yep, Jerry recently set a world record for stone skipping. Sort of makes him the Nolan Ryan of tossing rocks.

> **Jerry:** *We had the camera on the bridge filming down. We sent that to Rice University to the engineering department. They counted thirty-eight skips, and we forwarded that to Guinness. Within a couple of weeks, they wrote me a letter—they had accepted that as the '94 world record! Somewhere at the bottom of the Blanco is the Guinness world record stone of thirty-eight skips. And I'm glad that it's there, because I'd just as soon not have that. It belongs exactly where it is, at the bottom of the river.*

For Jerry skipping stones is more than a pastime. There's beauty and grace and power in it.

> **Jerry:** *I can throw a rock probably more than fifty or sixty yards, at most. But I can skip it 120. So it's a dance of the stone, and it's a very unusual and very interesting and very beautiful dance. It's a dance in the sense that the stone dances on the water, and you dance the stone from the shore to the water.*

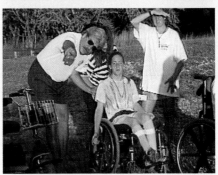

Jerry McGhee assumes that every human being, at one time or another, has bent over, picked up a smooth, flat, river rock, and sent it dancing across a body of water in a brief ballet between gravity and grace. While he is letting the world know about the fine art of skipping, he spends hours and hours with special needs children at the Texas Lions Camp in Kerrville.

> **Jerry:** *As long as you can use one of your arms, your upper arms, you can skip stones. And I intend to make people aware of it—both adults and children with special needs. When you approach any body of water, you approach as an equal with whoever is with you. I can't put into words what I get out of it. But I get something very deep out of it—a very deep satisfaction of bringing something to other human beings that I believe is important and interesting and athletic and healthy.*

There could be a child at the camp who might one day bump Jerry out of the Guinness Book of World Records. That, though, would only mean that he has succeeded in passing along what he considers to be an art and a dance, filled with the music of a half dozen gently fading water rings rippling across the surface of the Blanco River.

> **Jerry:** *When I see a child throw one skip and go into convulsions of happiness, it's just magnificent. To me, that's a big, big thrill.*

ROY BELLOWS' FORGE

Fredericksburg

Fredericksburg is a quaint little German community in the Texas Hill Country that is a perfect combination of its European and Western past. It's lariats and lederhosen, ten gallons and Tiroleans. It's the kind of place you never want to leave. And Roy Bellows rarely does, in fact, his office is just fifty steps from his front door. Fifty steps and a hundred years . . .

A map will tell you Roy Bellows' Blacksmithing Shop is located in Fredericksburg, Texas, in his backyard. And it is.

Roy: *I always wanted to have my workshop close to where I lived so I didn't have to commute a long distance. Didn't have to put on a business suit or put on an identity that wasn't part of my home life. Just walk out the back door and walk fifty paces and I'm at work, and I can get there any time of the day or night.*

But Roy will tell you it's found in the backyard of another century. It's a place where imagination and hard steel are hammered further into the past, back to a time when blacksmithing was seen as a magical mixture of craft and wizardry. Back to a time that still burns bright in Roy Bellows' forge.

Roy: *It's hypnotizing in a way, it's enchanting. It can be pure poetry . . . The smoke is rising, the flames are dancing, and the steel is doing what you want it to. Every hammer blow has an effect.*

Roy has never been big on horseshoeing. Never shoed one in his life. Roy wanted to take his craft a step forward . . . by taking a step back.

Roy: *Something that was made by the hand and has the evidence of the hand in it is beautiful. You can see the work that went into it. That's what I'm looking for—the old style, the old processes.*

It is no highbrow, low-stress career, this blacksmithing. Pounding iron day after day requires enormous strength and profound inspiration.

People ask Roy what one thing in his shop he couldn't live without. The answer to that is his graffiti wall. It's not for sale. It's something he did for himself. It represents the accumulated thought and random ideas of six years of working in this shop. Somewhere on there you will find the beginning of *Faust*, the beginning of *The Iliad*. *The Divine Comedy, Moby Dick,* Shakespeare, everything from world literature that he wanted to know about. It is Newton's law of universal gravitation to Kepler's laws of planetary motion. This wall opens up the infinite reaches of space. Space is something Roy thinks about a lot.

> **Roy:** *I wish people thought more about space. Fifty years from now, you know what I really want to be doing? I would like to be among the first colonists of the planet Mars. I'd like to forge out a new existence on Mars, the new frontier, the way we forged out a new existence in this frontier. I'd be willing to take that risk.*

Blacksmithing is Roy's life, but this threatens to be his creative legacy: a bed of nails. Two thousand in all, handcrafted and hot-forged over the course of a year.

> **Roy:** *Most people would question my sanity making this bed of nails, and I have to wonder sometimes myself.*

Now Roy is realistic enough to know his twenty-penny twin bed probably won't become the latest craze in home furnishings, but serious collectors are already paying serious cash for Roy's racks.

> **Roy:** *It feels like lying on a very hard surface. It's not particularly comfortable, but it's not uncomfortable either. Most works of art are more preposterous than this, and have no more useful purpose than this does. I like things that have an effect. A nail is definitely something that has an effect. So I made a bed of nails.*

Roy Bellows' forge and anvil may indeed be hidden in the backyard of another century. Back in a time when pounding hot iron was a privilege, and the blacksmith was a magician. Roy Bellows has found his place as part of that legacy, and he hopes when the smoke clears he has left a legacy of his own.

> **Roy:** *People must think that these things that I do, my wall, my bed of nails, my going to Mars, are strange and bizarre, but I think what is strange and bizarre is the people who stop dreaming.*

SINCE OUR STORY . . .

Roy Bellows is still pounding away in his backyard blacksmithing shop, only he now has a new apprentice—26-year-old Ezra is working side-by-side with his dad and plans to someday take over the family business.

WHEREVER TWO ARE GATHERED

Allen

I
t's a cold Sunday morning in Texas, one of those days when nothing would feel better than staying in bed, snug and warm under the covers, listening to that old north wind howl outside. And yet all across the state folks get up and get dressed and get themselves to church, rushing to have a seat in time for the sermon. But in small-town Allen, things are different.

George and Hazel Anderson are in no hurry. They know church would never start without them.

> **George:** *We have a duty to perform six days—on the seventh He rested. He asked us to give a reasonable portion of time, and so, on Sunday, I give it.*

It's just a little clapboard building, whitewash peeling from the walls. St. Mary may not look like much, but for more than a century this little church was the center of a community. Dozens of families gathered every Sunday for their weekly dose of faith and fellowship. But over the years folks moved away and passed on until one day the Andersons looked around, and they were all alone.

> **George:** *We used to have more people. We had a secretary of Sunday school, we had a secretary of the church, we had things like a youth choir.*

> **Hazel:** *It's not that we lost this church because of it breaking up. We've never had that type of disturbance.*

> **George:** *Majority of them passed on. The rest moved away. Kids grew up.*

For Hazel and George, St. Mary's is more than just a church. It's family, a constant shelter in a lifetime of storms, the place where they gathered with friends and neighbors and taught their children right from wrong. For the Andersons, this is where it all began.

> **Hazel:** *I met George here at the church. He used to sit on the right and I was on the left, and we would smile at each other. We were about fourteen years old, so we had a courtship—quietly.*

A lot has changed since those carefree childhood days. Time took its toll on this little country church. Each year was marked with another empty pew and fewer coins in the collection plate. Though the bells of St. Mary's fell silent long ago, every Sunday finds the Reverend Anderson right on time for the morning sermon. And always alongside of him is his wife. Hazel's the Sunday school secretary (without a Sunday School). She is also the church pianist without a choir. In fact, George and Hazel are the entire congregation, but they have the devotion of a multitude.

> **George:** *I come here because I never did believe in disbanding two things in life: the church and the school. We don't want this to be a disbanded church.*

There's just the two of them. Sunday morning services at St. Mary are by the book, the Good Book, of course. First, the Sunday school lesson, then on to record keeping, the offering, and finally the Reverend Anderson's sermon with plenty of that old time gospel thrown in. They don't need much, just a well-beaten Bible and an out-of-tune upright. Nothing that Hazel and George don't have at home, which might be a good place to be on a freezing Sunday morning. But the Andersons brave the ice and the cold to worship at St. Mary's—the tiny frame building that, for them, is as sacred as any cathedral.

> **Hazel:** *I don't understand how you would think that you are carrying out the Lord's command if you say, "Oh, it's cold today. I've got a good fire, I'll just say my prayers, get up, and do everything else that I want to do."*

> **George:** *Even if my wife is not able to come, I'll come down here and pray, until God calls me. As long as God is giving me strength and courage, I'll be here on Sunday. I feel like when it becomes necessary for God to add to the Church, we'll get more members. Until that happens, we'll just have to wait and do the part that we're supposed to do.*

The windows of St. Mary's are boarded up and broken. There will never be stained glass, plush carpet, or fancy chandeliers. And yet, in the purest sense of the word, this is a church, and these two lone souls are gathered in His name.

SINCE OUR STORY . . .

George and Hazel Anderson still attend their church every Sunday, but since our story ran, they now have frequent visitors join them.

THE GOOD OLD WAYS

MOVIES AT THE MAJESTIC
Wills Point

T he train doesn't stop in Wills Point, Texas, anymore. Like the rushing hands of time, it roars through town, leaving in its wake only distant memories of the way things used to be. The old bank, the soda fountain, a dry goods store. Back in the twenties, Wills Point had a family-owned picture show. One screen, on the square. It's good to know some things never change.

Karl: *We're the oldest theater in continuous operation in the state of Texas and perhaps even the United States. A lot of them been turned into opera houses or weekend theaters, but as far as movie theaters, I'm not familiar with many others.*

Karl Lybrand has seen a lot of opening nights here at the Majestic Theater. A lot of movies, a lot of memories.

Karl: *I can remember from a very, very young age, possibly even preschool, coming to the movies. I literally grew up here. And I was a real popular person because my brother and I both got to bring one buddy free.*

Karl Lybrand owns and operates the Majestic Theater just like his daddy did and his daddy before that. For three generations before the days of television and VCRs, before multiplex theater screens and $6.00 tickets, through wars and the Depression, the Majestic has endured. One screen, family-owned, in a town of 3,000.

Karl: *My grandfather started in the movie business in 1907 in Wills Point, and it has been in my family since, in continuous operation in my family since 1926—with modernization kept at a minimum, but doing the things that we had to do to stay in business.*

Repairs and painting are done catch-as-catch-can. Years of chewing gum cover the bare wood floor. Bricks peek out from behind cracked plaster, and the carpet is worse for the wear, but it's all part of the nostalgia that keeps folks coming back. And where else could you see first-run movies for three bucks?

Karl: *We want to keep the theater open as long as we possibly can. The touchups and the making things look cleaner are kind of part of staying in business. I don't feel the pressure of a deadline, that if it's not updated or improved by a certain time that it's a failure. We're doing some upgrading and modifications and cleaning up and painting. I feel comfortable here. Maybe it's because I can relate to my childhood. I've had people either from Wills Point or other small towns come up and say, "Gosh, this feels like when I was a kid going to the movies on Saturday afternoon." In the cities, when I went to the theaters—and they're beautiful when they're modern—I never felt quite as comfortable as I do here.*

In the Lybrand family tradition, Karl's wife, Kita, handles nightly ticket sales.

Kita: *Well, it came with the territory. Once he took over the theater, that meant I took over this job. That was just kind of the way it went. He relieved his dad, and I relieved his mom.*

Karl knew if he kept the Majestic Theater open, folks would continue to come. One night, with a little help from the caped crusader, Karl played host to a full house.

"BEFORE MULTIPLEX THEATER SCREENS AND $6.00 TICKETS, THROUGH WARS AND THE DEPRESSION, THE MAJESTIC HAS ENDURED. ONE SCREEN, FAMILY-OWNED, IN A TOWN OF 3,000."

Karl: *I really think it's important to the community as much as it is to my family because of the entertainment value and the few places there are for younger people and older people.*

Karl could have stayed in Dallas, sold insurance, and let the theater go. But with one look at a theater full of smiling faces, it's easy to see that Karl and his wife never really had a choice.

Kita: *I think if the theater were to close, it would be a loss to Wills Point. People don't think of it like that, because I guess they don't ever think of it closing. But someday it will probably have to close.*

Karl: *Selfishly, I think it's very important for this community, and I've had people tell me that—that they hope that it never closes. I wish the community had more things such as this. But I'm determined to make sure this one stays here.*

In the past seventy-five years, a lot of trains and a lot of time have passed by the Majestic Theater. But somehow it's remained open and unchanged. Karl Lybrand's granddaddy built this place, and now Karl is maintaining a family tradition by preserving an old movie house on the side of the tracks.

Bob: *Somehow, it's more than just a theater—it's a piece of history.*

Karl: *Well, it is to me. And I hope it is to the rest of this community. It certainly is a piece of history. You're right. There's a lot more here than just an old movie house.*

MUSEUM OF MEMORIES

Bradshaw

We spotted it out on a lonely West Texas road—the enormous old store and what I guess you could call downtown Bradshaw. We were in a hurry, but after one look inside, our schedule for the day had to wait. We were here to stay.

The woman who runs the only grocery store in Bradshaw, Texas, is Opal Hunt. Opal's father started selling groceries and dry goods here in 1905 when she was a child. But folks around here now know these groceries are not for sale.

> **Opal:** *I don't really call it a grocery store anymore. I don't think of it as that, really, because it's just a place for an old maid to stay, I guess. Over there I have crackers and popcorn. The other day there was somebody come in, picked up one of those popcorns. I said, "No, no we don't sell any more of those things. They're old."*

Groceries on the shelves, but they're not for sale. It makes you think storekeeper Opal Hunt has to be the worst merchant in the state.

> **Opal:** *Not anything for sale in here but sody pop and this old Washo down here. Now that's about forty years old. But I don't sell any more because that's gonna last me and that's the only washing powder I use. It's the best washing powder that I know.*

Along with the dozens of boxes of old Washo soap are memories—memories of a family that simply ran a grocery store in this tiny Texas town. Nothing is for sale. This enormous old tattered structure is a monument to a family.

Opal: *This is my mother's old cook stove. This is an old kerosene stove. She cooked for the public. I've tried to get all of her handiwork. I want you to look at that pineapple pattern in crochet and the fine thread. It's pretty messed up around here, but I mustn't make apologies 'cause that's the way it is.*

Bob: *Why do you keep all this stuff here like this?*

Opal: *Ahh . . . it's part of my life, part of me. Now don't ask what they are going to do with it when I'm gone. I can't be bothered about that because I'm enjoying it now. I'm really living now, because I never did treasure these things until now.*

Bob: *What brought about the change?*

Opal: *I'm a slow learner, does that answer it? I was always behind times. I was just slow about catching on. I'm really enjoying life now.*

Up and down the aisles in Opal Hunt's museum there are hundreds of moments frozen in time. The ceiling sags, and the floorboards creak, and, piece by piece, a vanished world is reconstructed with the old and not so old. It is an unfocused but unmistakable nostalgia, and Opal has learned that when you attempt to preserve the past, you discover its blessings and its short-comings.

Opal: *I believe in life, and I believe you should certainly enjoy what you have. As one of the kids around here said one time, "Opal, you live in the past." All right, if you don't have the past, you don't have a present, and you won't have a future.*

Bob: *When you sit here and look out across this store and see all these things that are the history of your family, and you think about all those old times and the time you spent here, what kind feeling do you get? What's the emotion behind all this?*

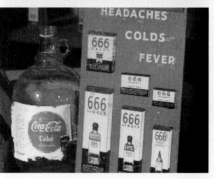

Opal: *Love, I love it! I think about Mama quilting on those quilts, cooking on the stove. I love it. I'm just as proud of it as I can be. There's a memory of my mother baking*

breads and my dad on the books. I'd stand by that old rolltop desk on his right an' I'd give him out the items that were sold that day while he listed it down in the ledger. Oh, I thought it was fun!

"I THINK ABOUT MAMA QUILTING ON THOSE QUILTS, COOKING ON THE STOVE . . . "

Bradshaw, Texas, where a woman named Opal turned a family grocery store into a family museum, a shrine to a way of life that can never be retrieved, where the forgotten past slowly emerges into memory.

Opal: *An old building with old things in it, that's a museum. I guess we just say that. Now when anybody brings anything else in here and wants to display it, I say, "Well, it wasn't ours." I say that I'm proud of my heritage, I'm proud to be a Hunt.*

SINCE OUR STORY . . .

Opal Hunt moved to a nursing home in nearby Winters, Texas, in early 2000. As of this writing, she still travels to Bradshaw occasionally to share her family story with passersby.

AMERICA'S BASKET FACTORY
Jacksonville

In the spring of every year, Martin Swanson becomes an emotional basket case. The pressure is on to somehow come up with hundreds and thousands of fruit and produce containers every day. You see, Martin operates one of the only basket factories left in America.

Martin: *We'll make anywhere from 6 to 14,000 baskets a day. I'm not sure how many that is a year, but it's a good bit. The timber used to make baskets is from local trees. That's why the basket factories are here, because of the trees—sweet gum, black gum, hackberry, birch, magnolia, cottonwood, elm.*

That old East Texas sweet gum is band-sawed, boiled, bent, and branded in this eighty-year-old factory where thousands of baskets are produced for the whole world every day. Even so, it's nothing compared to what it was like around this place in the old days.

Martin: *This is a round-bottom bushel basket. It's the exact same basket made the exact same way we've made it since the early 1900s. Not many changes at all. It survived the onset of cardboard boxes and plastic. We think that it's a container that will never be replaced. It's just an old process that hasn't changed much. I guess a basket and a clay pot were the very first containers used and they were in use in BC, so they've been around for a long time.*

Actually, Cherokee County's status as the basket capital of the world began at the same time the world developed a taste for what's known as the Jacksonville tomato.

Martin: *Back in the thirties it was considered the tomato capital of the world. In their heyday they would ship thousands of bushels of green tomatoes out every day. The first basket factory in Jacksonville was in 1898, and at one time I think there were five basket factories here in this area.*

But the tomato business went belly up after World War II. Before that

time, tomato farmers had their kids and everybody kin to them working in the fields. After the war, many of the younger people moved to different places, and a large part of the labor force vanished.

Martin: *The tomato industry just died on the vine, so to speak. Originally we sold the baskets to farmers, and they were used for farm use and pickin' fruits and vegetables, but now people use them in their homes. Somebody bought one today to transport a cat in. They put it in a basket and put a lid on it and took their cat somewhere. They're used for lots of different things. The design has just virtually stayed the same the whole time.*

If you've ever picked a peck of practically anything, most likely you hauled it home in a Jacksonville basket—bushels, bundles, pecks, part pecks, even painted pecks. Martin's found that people nowadays are buying baskets not for backbreaking field labor but for decorating their homes. It's just another sign of changing times.

This place is full of signs that times are changing. Part of the old factory has become a graveyard of sorts—worn-out basket benders are rusty and lifeless now. The old metal cries painfully with the slightest movement. These industrial antiques are a throwback to the steam era, when wide-open fields were ablaze with the red tomatoes and the woods were alive with the blowing whistles of the basket factories.

Martin: *Tomatoes grown in this area were known for their flavor. Good Texas black soil. It's a shame they're not grown like they were.*

Several years ago, Martin Swanson took over an industry most folks said was dying. What kind of person would hold on to this old factory, they'd ask. Well, thanks to Martin, the smell of the fresh-cut wood, the rhythmic sound of men and machines bending and weaving old East Texas timber has not become an echo of a forgotten past.

Martin: *I like the nostalgic appeal of the wood and the old machinery and the old process of making baskets. A lot of people just have a special place in their hearts for baskets.*

CANDY CREATIONS

Abilene

It's been said that we live in an artificial society complete with artificial ingredients, artificial coloring, and chemicals to substitute for the real thing. But in Abilene, Texas, we found a place where the people are as real and natural as their product. The place is Candies by Vletas. There's nothing artificial here.

George Vletas' father came to Abilene in 1912 and opened a business called Olympic Confectionery on Pine Street. Today George still makes candy the old-fashioned way, just like his mother and dad did. He still uses the same copper kettle and the same wooden spoons. He still dips the chocolates by hand. And he still uses only real and natural ingredients, making his candy twenty-five pounds at a time. George says this is the only way he knows, and he's not about to change things now.

. . . PURE CHOCOLATE, PURE SUGAR, TEXAS PECANS, AND PEANUTS, ALL HAND-DIPPED WITH PURE GOODNESS.

George: *We've been here seventy-eight years, here in Abilene producing candy. I figure I've got another good twenty years myself, maybe twenty-five years. My mother was ninety-two years old when she died, and she didn't quit work 'til she was ninety-one. Dipping chocolates and everything. So I've got thirty-one years to catch up with her now.*

Martha Vletas: *He is the mathematician—he does all that part of it. I'm the people person. If I don't recognize the face, they get grazing privileges. I usually ask if they've been in this store before, and if they say "No," I say, "Ah, you get grazing rights." So—they start sampling.*

These brightly covered foil boxes are filled with pure chocolate, pure sugar, Texas pecans, and peanuts, all hand-dipped with pure goodness.

George: *We sell energy. Our candy is full of energy. We don't count the calories, we count the energy factor. I like to see a finished product of*

what my employees do. I like to put my stamp on it for approval 'fore it goes out front to be sold or shipped to somebody.

Martha: *It's a business that brings a lot of pleasure to a lot of people, and that does make you feel good. You know that you have done something that pleases other people. When I married into this family, that was the thing that my mother-in-law taught me, that it's pleasure that you give to other people. My husband and I and our whole family are all proud of what we do, and we think we have done the best that we can do with candy. And the Vletas name is a name that I have always been proud of. When we put the sticker on it, we know we have sent out something we can really be proud of—that you'll like it when you eat it. You'll say, "Oh that's good."*

Tucked away on a street in Abilene, Texas, there is an old family business that sells a little bit of themselves with each piece of pure candy, and there's a family in Abilene that knows how to bring smiles to people's faces.

SINCE OUR STORY . . .

The Vletas are still making candy, but the business outgrew their old location. They are now part of the revitalization project going on in downtown Abilene, and have moved Candies by Vletas to a restored train depot.

CAR WASH WITH THAT?

El Paso

It is like an ancient morning ritual that still comes alive with every sunrise. There's been a hot pot of coffee at the H&H Car Wash and Coffee Shop every morning since the days when a tank of gas only set you back a couple of bucks. Long before microwave ovens, back when a hot meal came from a stove, this old neighborhood in the middle of the city was a place of comfort. It had a sense of belonging that made memories you could always come home to.

Maynard: *We bought it and opened in October of 1958. You need to change things sometimes, but if it's working, you don't need to change it. If you're successful the way it's going, then why change it?*

Yep, coffee shop and car wash. The old H&H has been like home for Maynard and Kenny Haddad since their daddy opened the place four decades ago. The only thing that's changed around here is—well, to be honest, not a thing.

Maynard: *I love it. I get up every morning at five o'clock, and from that time on, I'm ready to go. We've served millions of dishes at this place.*

Now that's a lot of slicing and dicing, waxing and wiping, stirring and steering over the years. Folks used to grab a bite inside while their car was being shined up outside, but somehow over the years the little twenty-two seat diner has earned an international reputation for outstanding fine Mexican cuisine. Even the locals can't keep it a secret any longer.

> **Maynard:** *That big-time cook whatever her name is that just turned eighty-something—Julia Child—she came in here and sat on one of those stools and watched that girl cook on that grill, and she couldn't believe it.*

> **Kenny:** *It's true, it's an old place. Restaurant reviews in the newspaper grade places A, B, C, and D, and whoever did this restaurant couldn't come up with a letter for us on decor and used the word "retro." I'm not sure what she meant by that, are you?*

> **Maynard:** *She means this place is antique!*

The H&H is a true living artifact of roadside America. In our changing world it's the stubborn survivor that proves new is not always improved.

> **Maynard:** *I was born right here. There used to be a house here, and I was born right in this spot. In those days you were born in a house.*

> **Kenny:** *When President Clinton was running for office, he went down this street, right in front of the car wash.*

> **Maynard:** *What does this place mean to me? Oh, I have to be careful because I'll get real emotional. I'm kind of a crybaby. This is my life. You know, you start with your dad and you end with your brother. That's what made us. Family.*

> **Kenny:** *We're still old America. We're not plastic.*

After so many years, it's still bumper-to-bumper outside and elbow-to-elbow inside. Folks in El Paso carry in their hearts a soft-spoken reverence for the H&H Car Wash and Coffee Shop. For them, and for Maynard and Kenny Haddad, it's a keepsake. It is a reassuring constant even after four decades.

EVERYTHING AND THE KITCHEN SINK

Mineola

There are two things that I especially like to do when traveling the back roads. One is to browse through old hardware stores in small towns, and the other is to eat. Well, there's a place in Mineola where I can do both.

A hundred years have passed down Broad Street since Kitchens Hardware first opened for business proclaiming, "If we don't have it—you don't need it." Today, there are still plenty of treasures hidden among the history. There are nuts, bolts, ten-penny nails, and twenty-gauge wire. As for the unusual, there are horn weights and something called a blab. When Jim and Bunny Young bought Kitchens Hardware, Jim figured the only thing it didn't have was a kitchen sink. So he built one and opened up a delicatessen right there in the front of the store.

Jim: *Have a seat, and if you're lucky, you'll get what you ordered.*

If you're looking for a hinge pin or a hex nut, Bunny will be happy to fix you up. But she won't fix you lunch. She's left Kitchens' kitchen to her husband Jim.

Jim: *My wife had never been in a hardware store, and she said, "I'd like to have this." And I was trying to find other things to do, and when she started to clean it up, I thought, well, I'd put a deli in. You can get a hamburger everyplace from Dallas to Baton Rouge, but you couldn't find a good sandwich. So I put this in and used local meats, and we just went from there.*

As far as we know, Kitchens is the only hardware store around that serves up a sandwich right next to the sandpaper. At first folks found it strange, but now it's the talk of the town.

**KITCHENS IS THE ONLY HARDWARE STORE
AROUND THAT SERVES UP A SANDWICH
RIGHT NEXT TO THE SANDPAPER.**

Jim: *It's the neighborhood bar with no alcohol. Everybody comes here, and we gossip and we tell things. Some of 'em are even true—the stories we tell—some of 'em aren't, but this is a good place to hang out. We're a dry county so it's our neighborhood bar.*

Bunny: *I think the first day that we were open, we sold three sandwiches, something like that. And it's just grown and grown from there. And it brings people from everywhere.*

Bob: *It's kind of funny—he runs the deli and you run the hardware.*

Bunny: *It's not really funny because I don't cook much, and he can't fix anything. When somebody comes in looking for hardware, they usually go to him because he's a man and he says, "I don't know, I can't find it. You'll have to go ask my wife."*

Bob: *And what if they ask you to fix them a sandwich?*

Bunny: *Well, I could, but they won't ask me again.*

Jim: *It's just a lot of fun being here, and when I'm out, I miss it too much. We try not to ever have anyone come in that we don't know 'em when they leave, and if we don't, then that's our fault.*

Whether you drop into Kitchens Hardware for a hacksaw and a hammer or a turkey on wheat, Jim and Bunny Young will serve you both combinations with a smile. The way they see it, a good sandwich is good for business, and business couldn't be better.

SCOOTERS ON MEMORY LANE

Canton

They lined America's back roads and blacktop highways back when traveling meant adventure. Full service wasn't something you paid extra for—it came as a courtesy. "Service with a smile," they called it. Seems somewhere along the way we traded courtesy for convenience. The days of full-service roadside filling stations may be a thing of the past, but Mike Merchant's making sure they'll never be forgotten.

Mike: *I remember, as a kid, old stations, and how they looked—the old Coke box out front, the old bench, and all kinds of old signs—and I just never completely forgot it. So when I came out here, well, I built that.*

Mike's station is authentic to the tiniest detail. Though it may look real, it's still only a replica. The signs are just for show, and the old pumps are empty. Mike's customers come here to refuel for a trip down memory lane. And for a fill-up of Mike's special expertise. His specialty is scooters—Cushmans, to be exact. More than a moped, not quite a motorcycle, Cushman was the standard among scooters for decades.

Mike: *Cushman started out building just a small engine, and then, later, it started producing scooters, back in the forties. They built 'em for the military, and they built 'em for civilian use. They were real popular.*

More practical than pretty, the Cushman was a cheap, reliable source of transportation for kids across the country. Kids like thirteen-year-old Mike Merchant, growing up in Wichita Falls.

Mike: *Back then, if I could get twenty-five cents for some gasoline, I could go a long time. All my friends had 'em. Everybody had a Cushman.*

Whether it was the arrival of imports or high-powered Harleys, the little old Cushman just couldn't keep up. Reduced to making industrial vehicles, even golf carts, the company finally dropped the line sometime in the sixties. These

days, the only place you can find them is in the junkyard in some old scooter scrap heap.

> **Mike:** *All I have sometimes is just a pile of rust. Very incomplete. Motors that have been setting for a long time—they're stuck, won't turn over. I get 'em in all kinds of conditions.*

Given little more than a bag of bolts and rusty wire, Mike restores Cushmans to their former glory. Most times, that means making parts and scrounging for others. He might do better to start from scratch, but the mechanic in Mike enjoys a challenge.

CUSTOMERS COME HERE TO REFUEL FOR A TRIP DOWN MEMORY LANE.

> **Mike:** *There's no such thing as a scooter that can't be restored. If you can get it to me, I can make it run. And the first thing I do is disassemble everything, sandblast it. Then we start back with the cosmetics on it—sheet metal you know. You just do a ground-up restoration on it.*

Mike points out a 1960 model Cushman Eagle with a modified engine, custom-made exhaust, and custom paint. A 1949 Cushman Pacemaker that was popular with kids because it had a back compartment where they could put their books.

> **Mike:** *This is a 1959 Cushman Eagle that I bought in an unrestored condition. I've had it for a number of years. You take a pile of rust, and it looks bad and has parts missing and you've never heard it run, and you get it all together and you fire it up. Everything works well—it feels pretty good. You're just out in the open in fresh air and going. You can see a whole lot. I just like riding.*

For Mike, that's what it's all about—with the wind in his hair and the road under his wheels. It's like a two-wheeled time machine carrying him back to the days when the Cushman ruled the road.

> **Mike:** *I remember going to the show, you know, parking out front—all the kids had their scooters there. Then going down to the root beer stand and finding some more of your friends, and they had their scooters. It was just a peaceful time. Kind of wish it were back.*

In his own small way, Mike Merchant is bringing back the good old days, from his classic filling station in Canton to his revival of the Cushman. Mike has rediscovered the fun and adventure of the open road.

NICK'S PLACE

Rosston

In less time than it takes to drive a big-city block, you can drive through Rosston, Texas, and see all there is to see. It wasn't always this way. Times were when Rosston had a gin, a saloon, four doctors, and a two-story hotel. Things have changed in Rosston, but one thing has not. The Rosston General Store is still in business, just like it has been since the day it opened back in 1879, and it is still the centerpiece of this community.

Nick Muller is the owner of the Rosston General Store. In fact, folks here now just call the store Nick's Place. Nick was born in Rosston. He's never left. He's keeping shop in this weatherworn reminder of the old days selling gas, groceries, and cattle feed. But the Rosston store is more than just a mercantile artifact. It's the lifeline of a tiny town that's still holding on.

Nick: *This is it. This is it for 8 or 9 miles around here. And folks here know I'm going to be here. Most all the time. And they come in to visit with me or to talk about feed prices or gas prices or how much taxes are. They know that they can come in and visit for a little while and kind of get away from what they're doing. You know, relax a little bit, sit around, and drink a coke, eat a candy bar or something like that, and visit for a while. And then they go on about their day.*

Bob: *That's pretty different from the big supermarkets in the big city, isn't it? Where they don't know you?*

Nick: *Well, you've been in 'em. Do you know anybody that works in one?*

Bob: *Can't say that I do.*

Nick: *All right, well here you get the whole deal. You get to visit with somebody and enjoy somebody's company and whatever. You get it all. You get the full meal deal here.*

More than anything, Rosston General Store is a gathering place for the forty-seven or so folks that still call this hamlet home. You don't even need a reason to stop by. There's plenty of shade under the roof's tin porch, and the bench out front is rarely empty.

Bob: *What do you talk about when you sit around here?*

Townsperson 1: *Crops, cattle, anything.*

Townsperson 2: *The weather'll be brought up before long.*

Townsperson 3: *This store holds the community together. Whoever runs this is the social worker, the minister if your soul's in trouble. He's the banker if you have money problems. He advises you. Most important man in the whole community is the owner of the store.*

In a way, Nick Muller is single-handedly keeping what's left of Rosston alive.

Bob: *Do you feel like you play a pretty important role in this community?*

Nick: *It's my home, and I try to make my community the best I can make it. I try to help everybody that comes in and out of here. I'm an only child in my family, and these are my aunts, my uncles, my cousins, everything. You're not kin to 'em, but they're just like family. I treat 'em like I'd treat my own family.*

"THEY COME IN TO VISIT WITH ME OR TO TALK ABOUT FEED PRICES OR GAS PRICES OR HOW MUCH TAXES ARE."

Spend some time at the Rosston General Store and you will quickly see that the glue that holds America together is not found in New York, in Washington, D.C., or in the nation's biggest industrialized city, but here, in tiny towns like Rosston, where people are born, grow up, marry, and manage to stay on to keep their community prosperous.

Nick: *When I was young, I thought about going out and exploring the world. But I got to thinking about this store. I wanted to keep on with the legacy. I didn't want just anybody to run it. These people are good friends. And I thought if I stick with it, they'll stick with me. And I don't know of any other job you can have that people will stick with you as long as you stick with them.*

More than a century since the Rosston General Store opened for business, Nick Muller is keeping alive a part of history. This centerpiece of a north Texas town is a place where all folks are family, and it's the only life Nick's ever known.

Bob: *How far have you traveled away from Rosston in your life?*

Nick: *Well, I've been to Antlers, Oklahoma. I've been to Canton—Texas, that is. And I've almost been to Amarillo. And I've been down south of Dallas just a little piece. And that's about it. Nowhere else. I haven't been anywhere else yet. There's a few places I'd like to see, you know, that I haven't seen yet.*

Bob: *Like . . .*

Nick: *Well, a person oughta go see the ocean, I think. Just kind of take it in. I haven't seen it yet. I might do that one of these days.*

And even if Nick Muller never does see the ocean . . . or make it all the way to Amarillo, we think he's seen the world. His world. A world he loves. A world you might not find anywhere else but right here, at the Rosston General Store.

RAISING THE ROOF

Nacogdoches

Back in the days of the early settlers, a barn raising was about the biggest social event of the year, with friends helping friends assemble a giant jigsaw of timbers, hand-cut from the wilds of a young America. But in the mid-1800s ten-penny nails and two-by-fours all but put an end to timber framing. And the craft never quite made it to Texas. Not until Tim Chauvin moved to the piney woods and set up shop.

At Red Suspenders Timber Framing, they may use electric saws and sanders, but the ways of the Old World are still very much alive. This is timber framing 1990s style.

> **Tim:** *Like all the masters in the past, we have taken the technologies available to us and applied them in their most advantageous form. When a power tool is used, it's used to remove a lot of wood in a hurry so we have more time to do the fine-tuning, which we do with hand tools. It's a 2,000-year-old craft. It's been developed all over the world, and it's been refined to the point where it's equated with art in most locations.*

Today this Old World art form is managed with the latest in modern technology. Plans are drawn on computers. Blueprints are spit out by high-tech printers. But it's the attention to detail that will keep Tim's timber-frame standing far into the future.

> **Tim:** *These types of buildings have histories in hundreds of years, not just decades. And it's nice just to go down in the shop in the morning and know that what you're doing, somebody's going to be able to see it several hundred years from now. It gives you a lot of responsibility. If it's gonna be there for that long, you better do it right, because folks are gonna have to deal with it long after you're gone. And we're hoping that they'll think good of us in two-to-three hundred years.*

The finished timbers are assembled near the banks of the Red River, far from Tim's Nacogdoches shop. This is where weeks of measuring, cutting, and sanding pay off.

Tim: *This is it. This is what it's all about. This is the culmination of everything we've done. We've cut all the pieces, and now the big trick is to see if they all fit together. "One, two, three, go!"*

The folks here to help all work for Tim. But not one of them knew a thing about timber framing before coming to his shop. They've learned by doing. Pioneers in a pioneer business. Friends helping friends.

Tim: *We've got folks with art degrees, geology degrees, biology, chemistry, physics. We even have a guy here who used to repair radar on aircraft carriers. So it's a strange mix. But it works. I don't know why exactly, but it does.*

It takes five men and one crane about four hours for a barn raising these days. But even a diesel engine belching black smoke doesn't rob the romance of it from Tim.

Tim: *I don't think it takes any of the romance out. The folks in the old days were doing the best they could with what they had. That's exactly what we're doing. We're just taking it a step further. That's the romantic part, really, taking what was there and improving upon it.*

Fran Boz is the anxious owner of a soon-to-be-barn. With any luck, it will still be standing when her great-great-grandchildren are here.

Fran: *There's something about thinking that this house will be there forever. And you know, it's not just walls. Some people like to hang art on a wall. I like the building to be the art. And it is.*

Tim: *It's worth something when you're done. It has a purpose, and it's creative at the same time. You can't lose. It's something you can look back at at the end of the day and say, "We did something."*

After about four hours, it's time to raise the roof. Months of planning and weeks of work all come down to this.

"IT'S NICE JUST TO GO DOWN IN
THE SHOP IN THE MORNING AND
KNOW THAT WHAT YOU'RE DOING,
SOMEBODY'S GOING TO BE ABLE
TO SEE IT SEVERAL HUNDRED
YEARS FROM NOW."

Tim: *What we've got to do is keep a 9,000-pound unit from twisting, and then land it in place in some mortises that none of these have ever met in their existence. So, it's kind of critical. Either it goes, or it doesn't go.*

It goes. With no nails and no fasteners, Tim Chauvin and a few of his friends built some history near the banks of the Red River. It was not a big social event. In fact, few folks even noticed. And the ones who did probably didn't fully understand what this was really all about. It was about a 2,000-year-old art form, and people working together to make something special. For Tim Chauvin, it was about taking the time to build something people will admire for a long, long time.

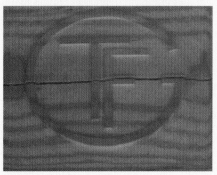

SINCE OUR STORY . . .

Red Suspenders Timber Framing continues to grow. Tim Chauvin and his team are now raising timber frames across the country. Tim also hosts a two-week timber-framing workshop held every other year at his Nacogdoches home. It's a chance for people to come and learn from the masters of the craft. Tim says the workshop has drawn interest from people around the world.

THE SWEET SMELL
OF WINTER

Troup

Shortly after the year's first freezing frost, the piney woods of East Texas are quiet. Nature takes her break, resting up for spring. But on one special day, the peaceful sounds of the wilderness are broken, and serenity surrenders to the joyful sounds of people.

There's excitement in the air, an electric current of anticipation married with the familiar smell of a wood fire. Friends and neighbors have gathered to swap stories while they stoke the fire and celebrate a traditional rite of winter. They have gathered at Gary Fields' family farm to cook ribbon cane syrup.

Gary: *This ain't syrup yet—it's close, just needs some fire. Some of the parts we have here are ours, some are borrowed. The whole community gets involved. It's just for the novelty of it—for the young kids to see it. And the old folks that grew up with this love to come out and spend the day. I guess it's kind of a dyin' art. There's not that many people that still know how, and we're just trying to keep it alive for the people that enjoy seeing it. It's certainly not for the money.*

"WE DO IT FOR THE FUN OF IT AND FOR THE APPRECIATION AND ALL THE PEOPLE THAT COME OUT AND HAVE A GOOD TIME."

It was just a few years ago when Gary Fields dusted off the old syrup cooker tucked away on the family farm. At the time, it seemed simple enough. You cut some cane, you squeeze it out and boil it down. Dozens of hours, and a lot of hard work later, Gary realized there's a reason the old cooker was left for scrap.

Gary: *I usually start about five o'clock in the morning, and we'll quit around six in the evening, and there's no stopping in between.*

Cooking good syrup takes time, practice, and a lot of patience.

Gary: *The mill that we use—the last year it turned before we started this operation was 1939. Syrup makin' has never regained the popularity it used to have and probably never will. We do it for the fun of it and for the appreciation and all the people that come out and have a good time. It's definitely worth it. We make almost enough money every year to go back in and do it again. There's not a profit margin at all in it.*

You might wonder why a man would go to so much trouble and not put a dollar in his pocket, but on Gary Fields' family farm this is not some business adventure or marketing scheme—you don't have to buy tickets and the conversation is free. The first-frost syrup cooking is about people and their heritage. It's about friends and family and East Texas tradition that you won't find anywhere else. Oh, and in case you come for the syrup, well, that's not bad either.

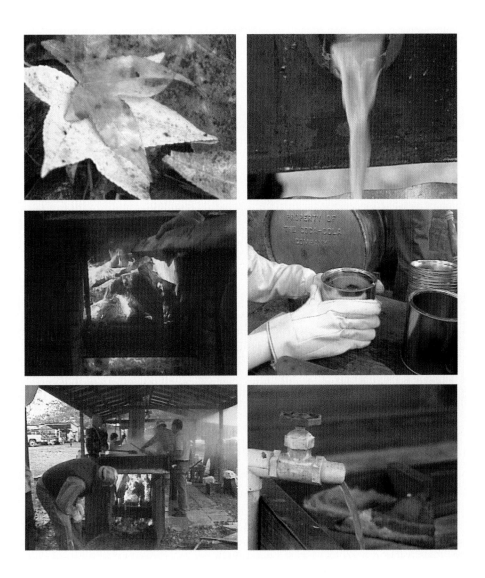

BLACKSMITH ON ICE

Whitehouse

e were toolin' down Highway 110 in Whitehouse, Texas, when we spotted it—a simple little building sitting right there, big as day, between Wacky Jack's Cafe and Mary's County Junk-Tion. It's the kind of place you might just pass on by, unless, like us, you are drawn in by the rhythmic sound of a blacksmith hammering out a careful cadence on hot steel.

Blacksmithing has been John Frederick's dream for the better part of his life.

John: *I've always had a passion for the old ways of doing things, and something told me, "This is it."*

John is what you'd call a modern-day blacksmith. Oh, he'd like to be forging out wagon wheels and plow blades, but today there's more call for candlesticks and fireplace tools. It's a little less romantic, but it's blacksmithing all the same.

John: *Seems to me I was born a hundred years too late. There's no wagons left to fix, so we got to do something. I fought the artistic side of it for years. I am not an artist, I am a blacksmith—just a dummy that hammers iron. Occasionally I get inspired and create something.*

"I SPENT THE FIRST HALF OF MY LIFE FREEZING AND THE SECOND HALF BURNING UP."

John has a bachelor of science degree from Purdue, and he spent twenty years managing steel mills before he decided he'd just had enough.

John: *I needed my own business and to do the things I really enjoy doing.*

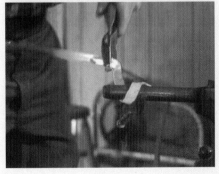

61

John Frederick is one of those guys who seems to have done a little bit of everything at one time or another. He's been an engineer and entertainer, a dancer and a clown. But his dream of the fiery forge was first sparked atop cold steel blades cutting across ice. John Frederick started out in life as an ice-skater.

John: *Yeah, I spent the first half of my life freezing, and the second half burning up. I started when I was three and skated seriously and competed. That was just another part of my life that I enjoyed.*

John was so good that he once toured professionally. Today, nearly thirty years later, he's still the hottest blacksmith on ice.

John: *Not too many people can tap-dance and blacksmith at the same time. 'Course I'm about a half bubble off level anyway. Just a labor of love— dance, skate, clown, blacksmith, all these things you can't make a living at. I guess in college you perceived art people as being in some other dimension of space and time, but that's not true, not true. I don't think that I'm a gifted artist—but I can jump out there and twist a piece of metal and have it look like something.*

Blacksmithing. It's all John Frederick ever wanted to do. Back in the days when he was gliding across the cold ice, back when he was an engineer in a sweltering steel mill, John Frederick wanted nothing more than to be a blacksmith. Like the red-hot glow of molten metal, it burned hot in his mind. Today, in a simple little building on Highway 110, John Frederick is pounding out a simple living with hammer, forge, and anvil.

SINCE OUR STORY . . .

John Frederick one day heard a voice that said, "Go west, young man," so he did. His new shop, Frederick's of Hico, is located at 118 North Pecan in Hico, Texas.

BLUE TIC INSPIRATION

Abilene

Folks have been known to hide their family heirlooms under the mattress, but the way Cecil Cox sees it, it's the Blue Tic Mattress stuffed with West Texas cotton that's the heirloom. Cecil says that any Texan worth his salt was born and reared on one. Never mind the modern innerspring, high-tech, computer-design support mattresses of the nineties. Cecil's family's been makin' these cotton-cram slumber bags for the better part of the century.

Cecil: *There's folks that will swear by these old cotton mattresses, and they'll never give 'em up.*

Larita Billups has seen her daddy, granddaddy, and everybody in between work in this little factory. As a baby she was serenaded to sleep with the rhythm of her grandmother's sewing machine.

Larita: *My grandmother taught me how to do this when I was probably in third grade.*

Every stitch has to be perfect, like the stroke of an artist's brush. That's what it takes for a small family business to last through so many generations. But lately it seems Larita's father spends most of the time working in the factory all by himself. Because when Larita's not stitching, she's sketching.

Larita: *Most people in town know of Old South Mattress Company. Whenever they say, "Where's your studio?" I say, "Well, do you know where Old South Mattress Company is?" Not every artist has their studio in with a mattress factory.*

When Larita Billups wanted to set up her studio and gallery, the art critics and highbrow buyers told her to choose a place of creative inspiration. Choose a quiet spot, a place where ideas come to you like a fine breeze. Well, the Old South Mattress Company was that place. It's now the world's only mattress factory and art gallery/art studio.

Larita: *First question people always ask me is where did I study. I never studied art, and I never took any classes for drawing. I just sat down one day and saw a picture that I thought would look really neat in black and white, and I set down with a pencil and started drawing and came up with an eagle.*

. . . A QUIET SPOT, A PLACE WHERE IDEAS COME TO YOU LIKE A FINE BREEZE.

It's in the mattress factory that she creates her detailed glimpses of nature, capturing emotion, strength, and the gentle side of wildlife—all the while her father's making mattresses and creating a commotion out back.

Larita: *When I'm drawing, I don't even hear what's going on over there. It's completely put out of my mind. Whenever he beats it out with that big long paddle, it almost shakes everything in the building. You can hear it all the way up here.*

Cecil: *Somebody asked me the other day how many mattresses I made in my lifetime. It would be in the thousands, and my dad, he probably made thousands.*

With Larita's help every day Cecil Cox pokes and punches these prairie sleepers just like his father before him. Cecil says there are really two artists here, each practicing a craft in the shadows of a longtime family tradition. Funny how inspiration can emerge in the back of an old dusty West Texas workshop.

MITT MAKER

Abilene

Brad Bailey works with leather, but it's not saddles or boots or belts he's crafting. Brad Bailey is making something very different. Something that in a way is more personal than either belts or boots, something that just might last a lifetime.

Brad: *Pretty much they come to me and then I show them patterns that I already have, and then we kind of just go from there. Most of the time they'll pick something that I've already got a pattern for, but, every once in a while somebody'll want something a little different. So we'll make an adjustment here, there, but most of the time, I try to get them to pick from the patterns I already have.*

In all our years of traveling we've seen folks make most everything, but never before have we seen, nor are we likely to see again, a man hand-cut, hand-sew, and hand-lace a custom baseball mitt.

Brad: *I think of it like a puzzle, putting a puzzle together. You got all these different pieces you're trying to fit in together to make something you can use.*

Brad got started making mitts when he offered to fix a broken glove for a friend. These days he's got enough work to keep him busy every night. But work comes catch-as-catch-can. This is just a hobby, and Brad doesn't have a shop on the town square. Brad's one-man assembly line is set up in the family dining room, and on a nightly basis Brad's in a race to finish what he can before dinner.

Brad: *Most of the time I can pick up pretty quick, and at least get it out of the way in time to eat. Sometimes we eat in the living room and wherever.*

It's a sign of the times how things that once were so ordinary are now so rare. Today the big glove companies turn out new gloves by the hundreds every day. Brad's production is slightly slower than that, but that's why we went to visit. Brad is one of a half dozen craftsmen in the country making gloves the old-fashioned way.

Bob: *Did you ever see yourself sewing?*

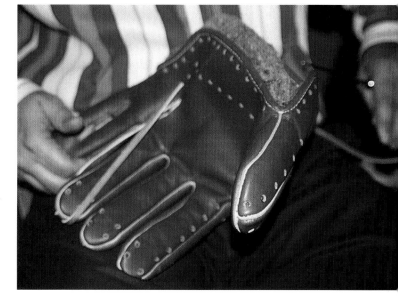

Brad: *No, I didn't. In fact, I didn't learn how until after I got the machine. I watched my mom sew, but I never sewed.*

You can bet the big glove companies don't steam their gloves over the kitchen stove, and they certainly won't take time to wrestle with every one, turning it right side out. But that's just the beginning of what handmade is all about.

Brad: *The gloves I make are all leather. I don't use any vinyl. I don't use any material except leather, except for the padding. So that's one advantage—you're getting an all-leather glove. The other advantage is you can design it a little bit the way you want it, be a little more specific about what you want. You know what type of web you like, that kind of thing. Also you can get your name either branded onto the glove or monogrammed in the glove, and it kind of makes it more of a personal glove.*

More than a piece of sporting equipment, a good ball glove can become a personal treasure. Remember the smell and feel of your first glove? Brad remembers his, and he hopes his gloves will also make memories.

Brad: *Some of the people—you're kind of wondering if they are gonna take care of it. Are they gonna keep it clean, will it last long enough to maybe give to their grandkids. Some kids' favorite glove becomes like their favorite Teddy Bear or something. I've had a couple of kids bring their gloves by to be fixed, but they hated to leave it here and not have it with them all the time.*

There was a time when all gloves were handmade. Mass production and automation changed all that. Brad Bailey, though, has the time and the patience for the old ways, and somehow he's worked his way into handcrafting functional works of art that can stand the test of time.

Brad: *Take good care of a glove and keep it clean, and it ought to last a good long time. Kind of depends on how many games you play with it. I'm trying to make a glove that will last.*

SINCE OUR STORY . . .

Brad Bailey's daytime job required him to move to Plano, Texas, but he's still making mitts on the dining room table when wife Sandy will let him have it.

PINE MILLS POTTERS
Mineola

They say that over the last half century more and more people have moved out of the country and into the big city. We're happy to report that there are plenty around that have moved the other way—like the folks that call themselves the Pine Mills Potters.

There are other things Gary and Daphne Hatcher could be doing for a living. He knows the construction business, and she has been in sales. But from the day they met in school, they knew their lives would end up in clay.

> **Gary:** *I think, ultimately, everybody has to create, and clay seemed the most appropriate medium for me to channel my creativity through.*

> **Daphne:** *I like to tell people that we just never passed the mud pie stage of development. That's where we're stuck at, and that's what we still like to do—make mud pies all day long.*

When Gary and Daphne first built their kiln up on the hill, there was no building around it. Folks mistook it for a barbecue pit and stopped by all the time, wanting to know when the rib stand would be opening up. When they learned Gary and Daphne were potters, folks didn't know what to make of it.

> **Daphne:** *Gary joined the volunteer fire department, and he'd say, "What do you do?" and the guy would say, "I'm an oil field worker" or "I'm a welder," and they'd say, "What do you do?" and he'd say, "I'm a potter." And they just wouldn't even know what to think about it. No one related to what a potter was. I don't know what they thought we did.*

When they came to the piney woods, Gary and Daphne felt drawn to the place, but they didn't know why. Now they think they do. It seems they weren't the first potters to call Pine Mills home.

> **Daphne:** *When we were starting on the lake, and the bulldozer uncovered a large pile of potsherds, we . . .*

Gary: *We said, "Stop! We want to look."*

Daphne: *"Stop" is exactly what we said because we didn't know what else would be there. We didn't want anything else disturbed—as you walk over the dam of the lake, there are just potsherds everywhere. Every square foot is covered with pieces of brick and pieces of potsherds.*

WHEN YOU TAKE HOME A PINE MILLS POT, YOU TAKE HOME A LITTLE PIECE OF EAST TEXAS.

What they had found was the remains of a kiln dating back to the Civil War. And every broken jar and jug is a piece of the potters' history.

Gary: *The sheer irony of potters settling in Pine Mills and then finding an unknown pottery on their property—we were just amazed, absolutely amazed. But these people, they didn't see themselves as artists. They were just trying to feed their family. They probably made pottery and traded it for other services, traded it for a mule or traded it for some blacksmith work. Sometimes I think that what we do is kind of difficult, but these people, they had to dig all their own clay. They had to build all their own equipment. They were truly primitive potters. It makes what we do look a lot easier.*

Gary and Daphne like to think that when you take home a Pine Mills pot, you take home a little piece of East Texas. The kiln is fired with East Texas pine. The pottery is made with East Texas clay. Even the handles in the serving trays come from the East Texas muscadine vines wrestled from the trees.

Gary: *Of course, you see stickers on everything these days that say "Handmade." Most of it's not. There are a lot of potters that make mass-produced pottery, but sensitive people can tell the difference. I think that's one reason that people buy our work, that our work has sold as well as it does.*

They could have done something different. Gary could have stayed a carpenter. Daphne could have stayed in sales. We're happy to report they didn't.

Gary: *We're just both trying the hardest we can to materialize our dreams.*

ACCORDION ROSE

Port Aransas

Accordion Rose is a reluctant heiress to a musical legacy that started years ago in a storefront in Ohio and ended up down on the Texas coast. She's one of the last folks around with the Old World knowledge of a very unordinary instrument.

Rosie: *This is a special little recipe that I'm cooking up. One batch will last for two years. But ah, when you get it all cooked together and it comes out the perfect color, I'm so happy for two years. Because that's how long it normally lasts me, about two years. That's my secret sauce. It has to cool down before I can use it. You can't smell that?*

It's no reflection on her cooking, but Rosie Ridgeway has stirred up a crazy concoction in her kitchen so odd that it will sit here for two years and no one will ever take a bite. But when it comes to fixing broken accordions, Rosie's secret sauce is a magical mixture that holds it all together.

Rosie: *Oh, listen to that. That one's got problems! Sounds terrible! It doesn't bother me but it bothers my husband to death. He's in another room and he has to listen to that eeee, errr, eeee, errr. It's like—oh, my God . . . close the door!*

Nope, Rosie's recipe ain't for eatin', but her iron skillet creation will go to good use. Back in the spare bedroom, back where you might expect to find a quilt shop or a sewing room, Rosie Ridgeway is making repairs on one of the most unique musical instruments ever created.

Rosie: *My father had the last accordion factory in the United States that made accordions from scratch. It was in Toledo, Ohio.*

Accordions have been a part of Rosie's life as long as she can remember. In fact, it was her daddy, Al Trick, who directed a nationwide network of accordion schools after his days on the vaudeville stage. It was the 1950s, and accordion music was a hit around the country and on the airwaves until . . .

> **Rosie:** *Elvis Presley. Elvis Presley came on the Ed Sullivan Show and shook his hips with this guitar and that was the end of the accordion era. It died that evening. After that all the kids wanted to play the guitar. None of them wanted to play the accordion.*

Almost overnight the accordion became a musical relic, but forty years and a lot of musical history has passed. From the dusty depths of basements, closets, and attics, the accordion has once again emerged. They are antiques, family treasures. The lucky ones find their way to Rosie, who has a way with the rhythm box.

> **Rosie:** *These people, they'd say to me, "What happened to that little girl that worked in the back there in the shop with them?" I'd say, "I'm the little girl that worked back there in the shop . . . It's me!" And people are so glad they found me. They say, "Ah yes, I remember coming in there and talking to your dad. He was such a sweet old man." And they say, "Rosie, you're going to take over this, aren't you?" And I say, "No, didn't plan on it." "But who's going to do it?" they'd ask. "You know how to tune. You know how to take them apart and put them back together. You know how to do all this. Who's going to do it—fix accordions?" And the more I got thinking about it, I knew they were right. You know anyone else can do this?*

"I'M THE ONLY ONE IN THE FAMILY THAT DIDN'T PLAY THE ACCORDION."

So that's when Rosie got another house with a garage conversion, put the shop in her house, and opened up as Accordion Rose.

> **Rosie:** *It's been unbelievable! People are still finding me. So now I'm doing accordions full time and never ever thought that I would have this job, never in a million years. There's always jokes about the accordion. This accordion player was so worried about leaving his accordion in the car because it was gonna get stolen. And when the accordion player came back to the car there were two more in there!*

One thing we've learned in our travels is that not every artist is a musician. We've met guitar makers who didn't know a C chord from a C-note, a tone-deaf violin maker, and a harp maker who didn't know the first thing about playing the harp. Add Rosie to the list.

> **Rosie:** *"You're called Accordion Rose and you don't play the accordion? Aw, come on!" They think that's my stage name. I'm the only one in the family that didn't play the accordion.*

Rosie Ridgeway is one of the last who can prevent the accordion from becoming just an off-key heirloom.

> **Rosie:** *Sometimes I get the feeling that there is an accordion in everybody's attic in the whole state of Texas. And one way or another it's gonna end up on my bench.*

SINGING DRYWALL MAN
Greenville

There are certain men with little want, need, or attraction to the bright lights of stardom. Big Bill Johnson is such a man. Big Bill took a chance at fame and fortune in Nashville, Tennessee, but he traded it for a bucket of mud and a drywall knife in Greenville, Texas. Meet Big Bill, singer, songwriter, and drywall man.

Bill: *It keeps me fit. I work by myself, and I write a lot of songs. I get a lot of song ideas when I am out working by myself. I wrote a song one day when I was out on the job—"I used to believe in you, but now I'll be leaving you." And that's all it took. I've had a lot of great ideas doing drywall.*

Big Bill Johnson is one of the busiest country music singer-songwriters this side of Nashville. For years, he's been known only as Big Bill. But word of his day job has gotten out, and Bill's now the state's only "singing drywall man."

Bill: *I've got that title. I tell you what happened. I was doing drywall, an' the guys kept saying, "Why don't you write a song about drywall?" So I thought, "Well, I will one of these days." I ain't caring about everybody and their brother knowing I do drywall and work in music too.*

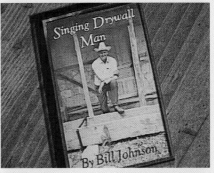

Bill's album probably won't put him in the spotlight, but it's a place he's not unfamiliar with. He's rubbed elbows and played guitar with some of the greats—Loretta Lynn, Johnny Cash, Boxcar Willie—but Big Bill turned down a record contract and moved to Greenville, where he could write simple country songs about his simple country life.

Bill: *I write just pure country. I am country. I get my ideas from all different places, reading the newspaper, newscasts, and just about everything. Some of 'em are just direct from God, I guess. I'm just walking along, or maybe just get out of bed in the morning*

and something will just pop into my head just like there was a radio on in there or something. I love it. I just like doing music and drywall. Both of those things are just a part of my life.

Big Bill's not sure how many songs he's written. He stopped counting at a thousand. But more than a hundred have been recorded. And a few have been hits. And it all started as a way to avoid barroom sing-alongs.

Bill: *We used to work in these clubs all the time. Well, you'd be in the club, about eleven or twelve o'clock at night, an' everybody'd get a few belts in 'em. They'd all want to come up and sing. So I said, "I know how to stop this. I'll write my own songs."*

Down at Pickle Brothers' Lumberyard, they've got Big Bill's drywall supplies and one thing he won't find at Wal-Mart—the hardware rehearsal hall for a little group called Pickles Pickers. It's a place where Big Bill's still a star.

Bill: *Oh, I tell you these guys are something else. We get over there, oh, once a week or so and just pick and sing and have a good time. I wrote a song called "The Good Old U.S.A. Way of Living," and those guys just love it. I love to play music, and if anybody will listen to me, I'll just pick and sing as long as they will let me do it.*

Big Bill Johnson stepped out of the Nashville spotlight and stepped into a place where he's comfortable—Aisle Four at the Pickles Brothers' Lumberyard, a great place for a drywall man.

Bill: *Pickles' Lumberyard is a long way from Nashville, and I'm glad of it. This is as close to Nashville as I want to get. To get me in Nashville, it'd take six of these strong guys carrying me there. I'd be fighting every step of the way.*

"SOMETHING WILL JUST POP INTO MY HEAD JUST LIKE THERE WAS A RADIO ON IN THERE OR SOMETHING."

THE VOICE OF THE TREES

Groveton

Germany's Black Forest has nothing on East Texas. Fact is, the national forests in Texas are some of the thickest woods anywhere in the world, and the kind you'll see more than any other is the good old southern yellow pine. They're as common as ticks on a ranch dog here, but other than making great two-by-fours for building a house, there's really nothing special about them. Or so we thought. That was before Maria Minaar taught us a lesson about the yellow pine.

Maria Minaar grew up in Zimbabwe, the child of a missionary. It was in Africa that Maria learned to make and play a musical instrument called the marimba, which was crafted from a rare African wood.

> **Maria:** *It sounds like a tree, like the voice of a tree. That's the best way I can describe it. Some people have wondered what they were and where they came from. People love the sound of them.*

When she moved to East Texas, Maria found that the southern yellow pine—the good old common-as-ants East Texas yellow pine—provides a tonal quality that

rivals the finest traditional marimba ever made in Africa. Her mission now is to let the rest of the world listen to this voice that comes from the trees. It is here in the midst of Texas' piney woods where Maria makes marimbas.

> **Maria:** *It's really inspiring to live out here in the woods. I can go out, and I can play as loud as I want and as much as I want and in the middle of the night if I want, and nobody cares because the neighbors can't hear it.*

But it wasn't long before folks started following this strange sound all the way through the woods to Maria's front door. Now Maria not only makes marimbas, she teaches others how to play them.

> **Maria:** *It sounds like a madhouse in there sometimes when everybody's practicing, but it works fine like that. Don't ask me why—it just works. Some of them have never played a musical instrument in their life. It's wanting to perfect what you're playing, but also, just the neat feeling of beating something with sticks as hard as you want to. The louder you beat on it, the better it sounds.*

Somehow, without a fiddle or guitar in sight, these new musicians have developed quite a following in East Texas. With concert dates filling up the schedule, and even a CD out in the stores, the Groveton Marimba Band is probably the only football halftime marimba band in the world.

> **Maria:** *I have a hard time peeling them off the instrument at the end of practice, so I know that they like it. And it's very rhythmic, very moving, and most kids really seem to like that.*

Maria Minaar's never alone in her workshop, she says, because she's in the company of ancient voices. The music carries her back to Africa.

> **Maria:** *It bypasses the mind and goes straight through the ear into the heart. It makes me think about Africa. The smell of a cooking fire in the night from the village nearby, or the sight of the huts out in the rural areas, or just people moving about in the streets. One of the things that this music does is to bring that back.*

WILDWOOD DEAN

Bonham

Some men have neither use nor care nor craving for what we call the easy way of life. They are folks who, quite simply, feel at home with what nature can provide. Dean Price is such a man. We met him in the icy bogs and bottoms on a late December day, going after the dogwood destined for his workshop.

Dean: *We used to fish and hunt up and down these bottoms. My granddad moved here in about 1845 or somewhere around that time. And then we moved to the river in 1947. All my childhood was spent on the river. We was just basically living off the land.*

The river is the Red River. Along its banks and in its hollows is where Dean Price's family lived out what they called the D-days: drought, dust, and Depression.

Dean: *Times were hard, but I didn't realize that the times were hard. Fish and beans were our staple food. And it was good providing. It wouldn't provide you with enough money to go buy a new car and things like that, but it provided you with the necessities. We had plenty of food at all times, from the things we raised and from the river. I'll always remember those times running up and down the river and the things we did on the river.*

Childhood memories are hard to shake and Dean Price has never bothered to try. In those D-days, his dad made his living building fishing nets from dogwood branches and cotton string and selling them up and down the river. Dean grew up and roamed a bit. He tried the city and came on back, back to the river, back to the dogwood. Just like his daddy did.

Dean: *It's hard to get. You've got to get down where it grows, down on the other side of the tracks to find it.*

The main thing about the dogwood, it's a real hard wood, almost as hard as hickory. It's been used for bobbins and golf club heads and mallets. A lot of the old cotton spindles were made from dogwood. It'll bend, it'll make a good bend.

Now these days you've got your aluminum and your fiberglass, and there's no more call for wooden fishing nets. But the dogwood still provides in ways that Dean's dad never saw.

Dean: *I think about it a lot, how he went through all those years of using dogwood for net hoops and never did build anything. Never did build any furniture.*

In his workshop near Bonham, Wildwood Dean Price designs and builds dogwood twig furniture. This is not the flowering dogwood you see in East Texas. This is more of a mongrel dogwood. But what it lacks in color, it makes up for in strength. Dean figures the screws will give out long before the dogwood does.

Dean: *It's gonna be real sturdy furniture that's gonna last a lifetime. Especially indoors. Now if it's left outdoors, it might not. But indoors, there's no telling. It'd last a hundred years, I guess. It's such a tremendous satisfaction to me to design my own furniture and to go into the woods down on the river, where I love, and gather the material and come into the shop with a pile of sticks and wind up with a beautiful piece of furniture. I never cease to stand back and look when I get through at what my pile of sticks has made. It usually looks real good to me.*

For the people who want this backwoods furniture—people who find it more appealing than plastic and glass and steel—but don't care to flog the Red River bottoms themselves, Wildwood Dean's put out a catalogue. A country catalogue, written, typed, and published by Dean Price. It gives Dean Price a way to tell the story of his life. Of how his father worked hard and raised a happy family out where the wildwood grows.

"ALL MY CHILDHOOD WAS SPENT ON THE RIVER . . . JUST BASICALLY LIVING OFF THE LAND."

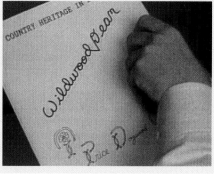

Dean: *Yeah, my dad taught me to never let external forces bend you against your will. He was a firm believer in being your own person, and when I was young, he wouldn't let me follow the trends and the fads of the other kids. He wanted me to be my own person, and I take that from the dogwood. You can't bend dogwood against its will. It'll snap and break. And that's my motto. Just never let external forces bend you against your will.*

LONE STAR LEGACY

A GIANT OF A MAN

Huntsville

e tend to stick to traveling the back roads, avoiding the speed and convenience of the interstate for good reason. We find it hard to sightsee when the scenery is zipping by at seventy miles per hour. But we did find one sight on I–45 that got our attention. Demanded it, in fact. General Sam Houston towering over the highway in Huntsville!

Gene Pipes of Huntsville knew the state needed something big to celebrate Houston's 200th birthday. What he got was the tallest statue in the state. At 67 feet tall on a 10-foot base, it's a larger-than-life tribute to a larger-than-life man.

Gene: *The thing is, that ten-times life size is particularly Texanish. He was bigger than most of the men of his time. He was a man completely ahead of his time.* The Tribute to Courage, *as it is named, was intended to recognize the amazing accomplishments of Sam Houston himself. He came to Texas and saved the republic from absolute destruction by winning the Battle of San Jacinto. He went on to be president of the republic, governor, senator. He's somebody to be reckoned with in our history.*

"HE WAS BIGGER THAN MOST OF THE MEN OF HIS TIME."

It took a big imagination to create such a grand statue, and Huntsville native David Addict's imagination was as big as his respect for Sam Houston. So with a little time and a lot of effort and thirty tons of concrete, David commemorated the first president of Texas.

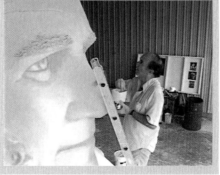

David: *Sam Houston's always been a hero to me. Tallest sculpture of an American hero. The other two taller ones are the Statue of Liberty and a saint, a religious figure in Butte, Montana. So Sam is going to get his glory, finally.*

It was like an old-time barn raising. The folks of Huntsville rallied around and gave their money and hearts to stand with Sam. Together with David, they

raised a monument so the world and the drivers on Interstate 45 could share in the honor of a Texas hero.

> **Gene:** *We've had visitors from sixty-four nations, and every state in the union. Over 100,000 people have come to this site since it was dedicated October 22, 1994. Remembering our heroes is important, because our society today needs to remember badly where we came from and what we are. This makes history alive. It makes it part of what we are and part of the fabric of the state.*

A giant statue of a giant man in a giant state.

DIVIDERS OF THE PLAINS

McLean

elbert Trew has spent most of his life in McLean, Texas, fascinated with two things. One is barbed wire. The other is Route 66. Together they shaped the history of the rough and rugged land of the panhandle plains. Now he's making sure that that history is not forgotten.

Delbert: *Probably one of man's basic instincts is to say, "This is mine. You stay off." So, barbed wire allowed the settlers to, in a very unique way, control the use of their land and also show where their boundary and their property was.*

Barbed wire—that twisty, prickly metal that cut the panhandle prairies into pieces. It's been blessed and cursed for more than a century. Proper folk called it "the devil's rope," because it harmed the livestock. Homesteaders praised it, because it kept the longhorns on the drives north out of their crops.

Delbert: *Actually barbed wire was what really made it possible to settle the West and give control over the prairies. We think barbed wire settled the West more than six-guns and the sheriffs. I would say that half of the cowboy's time is spent repairing or building or rebuilding or doing something concerning barbed wire.*

Delbert Trew's other fascination divided the plains in another way. Twisting and winding its way through towns from the north to the Pacific coast, cutting a swath through the dusty Texas panhandle, is Route 66—or at least what's left of it.

Delbert: *We like to call it the mother road, because everybody just kinda fled to the road, hoping the road would take them to better times and better things in their life. We have generation after generation here that made a living, educated their children off of the tourists right here on 66, so it has lots of fond memories.*

Delbert Trew is the manager of memories at the Barbed Wire and Route 66 Museum in McLean, Texas, where visitors can see examples of barbed wire from around the world and memorabilia from Route 66—reminders of a not-so-distant past.

PROPER FOLK CALLED IT "THE DEVIL'S ROPE," BECAUSE IT HARMED THE LIVESTOCK. HOMESTEADERS PRAISED IT, BECAUSE IT KEPT THE LONGHORNS ON THE DRIVES NORTH OUT OF THEIR CROPS.

Delbert: *They're coming back. They're wanting to retrace where they've been. It was their flight from the Depression, and the dust bowl was such a traumatic thing that it really left an impression upon their minds, so these people are traveling back.*

They are traveling back to a time when you brought your own bedding to stay at the local tourist court for two dollars and fifty cents, a time when you didn't need to rehydrate your eggs. They were cracked fresh over the griddle.

Delbert: *A lot of our young people today are getting real tired of plastic. They are getting tired of the fast track. They are kind of coming back to the old real nitty-gritty of things. And this is one part of history that they can really witness and go over again and really relive. We wanted to show life was harsh, life was hard, and barbed wire definitely is one of the things that shows how harsh the environment really was.*

In the panhandle plains, Delbert Trew is making sure that the people who built and made their living in these two periods of history won't be forgotten.

GHOST TOWN NO MORE

Gruene

ruene, Texas, is nothing more than the intersection of Gruene and Hunter Streets, just north of New Braunfels. The speed limit is somewhere between slow and easy. For a half century, Gruene was a ghost town, a wisp of cobweb on some old forgotten road map. But it hadn't always been like that. Gruene was a busy place for a while. Crops were ginned at the Gruene family mill, and farm hands traded at the family store. Then things went bad.

For forty years after the Depression hit and the cotton died, the once bustling buildings did little more than whistle in the wind. The founding Gruene family even gave up on the place. But Gruene didn't stay that way. Strangers came and turned the town around. Pat Molak, an unhappy stockbroker from San Antone, was one of the strangers.

> **Pat:** *I wasn't a very good stockbroker. I couldn't call a guy if I sold him a stock and it went down. I wasn't a tough enough salesman.*

In 1974 Pat and some partners heard about a ghost town by the Guadalupe that was about to be bulldozed for riverfront condos. Pat and his friends stopped by for a look and have been here ever since.

> **Pat:** *About mid-twenties the Gruene family— they were in the cotton farming business—ran into the boll weevil and the Depression about the same time, and it kind of just killed the town. And the main namesake of the town, H. D. Gruene, died right in that era too. So the town really just came to a halt about 1925, 1930.*

Little by little, Pat and Company got it moving again. They helped fix the old place up. And little by little, the tourists trickled in. The old H. D. Gruene Mercantile became an antiques store. Out back, the old storage barn is a potter's shed. Even the tumbled Gruene Gristmill has been converted to a restaurant, and the once decrepit Gruene mansion has been restored as a family inn.

Little by little, the town has recaptured almost half a century. Pat's had a lot of help along the way, mainly from his partner, Mary Jane Nalley.

Pat: *Mary Jane was a banker and so we were strictly legit—coat and tie every day. We were fortunate enough to come along at the right time, right when they put up the dance hall for sale. And that's how we got started. We bought the old dance hall.*

Half a century ago, a local farmer climbed to the top of the water tower, took one last look around at the wasted fields and the dying town, and hanged himself, thinking Gruene was gone forever. That story is legend now. The sun has come out on Gruene, Texas, again. New paint, new business, new life.

Bob: *What do you think we would have lost if this place had been demolished?*

Mary Jane: *A lot of fun and a lot of good times, for one thing. There's a certain charisma about the town that people talk about—that the Gruenes must have been really nifty people because there's a certain feeling here. That would have been gone. It's not just the buildings.*

Pat and Mary Jane credit the developers who sold this town to them with saving the place. They realized its significance and decided not to tear it down.

> **Bob:** *Do you think the town can get overrestored?*

> **Pat:** *That can happen. We're doing our best not to let that happen. We have acquired most of the real estate around Gruene ourselves, and if we can hold onto it, we're going to do our best to make sure that doesn't happen.*

Now every year at the Gruene Hall honky-tonk, they have a little bash, a celebration of a town that's back on the map, thanks to a couple of strangers that came its way.

CHARCOAL COWGIRLS

Frisco

We meet a lot of storytellers out on the back roads. People who share a bit of themselves through words or music. Donna Howell-Sickles tells a story every time she picks up a piece of charcoal and starts to sketch a scene. Lines and colors intersect to tell the story of a western way of life and the women who were part of it.

More than twenty years ago, Donna Howell-Sickles ran across an old postcard depicting a real western cowgirl of the 1920s. Complete with costume and trick horse, this cowgirl triggered an image in Donna's mind, and her life has never been the same.

Donna: *The appeal to me was that it was an obviously invented image. But it was an image that I felt like a lot of us had pretended to be at some point, playing cowgirls ripping up and down the alleys.*

Now, in her Frisco studio in an old Texas farmhouse, she continues to breathe life into her charcoal creation. For Donna, the image of the cowgirl is not just a pale imitation of the cowboy.

Donna: *As she evolved and I became aware of the women who helped create this image, the women of the Wild West shows of the teens and early twenties, I became fascinated with them, with their personalities and how atypical they were for their time. And the kind of raucous zest for life they had. I use the cowgirl to show the strength and the humor that all women are capable of. It's something we all aspire to—kind of just a joyous embrace for the whole act of living.*

Capturing the images dancing in her mind has never been difficult for Donna. Even as a child, growing up on the Red River, Donna found ways to express her ideas. While other kids dabbled in finger paints, Donna used the juice of mashed up pokeberries to spice up her creations. Always the adventurous one, Donna found the walls of nearby caves to be the perfect canvas for her artwork. From the caves of north Texas to some of the hottest galleries of the American Southwest, Donna's captivating cowgirls have won the hearts of art lovers.

Donna: *I've had openings where the guys have told me, "I want to meet her—I want to meet someone just like that." That sounds really healthy to me. To think that something that you draw can make somebody else stronger as well. That's a great thing.*

Donna's images are filled with myths, memories, and legends, stories intertwined from the past she hopes will inspire events in the future.

"I USE THE COWGIRL TO SHOW THE STRENGTH AND THE HUMOR THAT ALL WOMEN ARE CAPABLE OF."

Donna: *The idea that I get to be a storyteller, that I can tell such a powerful story to people that I don't even get to meet, is appealing. And when I'm really working on a deadline to get things done for a show, telling the stories is what can pull me out of bed at four o'clock in the morning. The images can get me out here.*

Donna's far from finished with telling the story of her cowgirl. The creation keeps growing and changing right along with her creator.

Donna: *She's tied very much to how I perceive the world. As I go through growth, the women in my images do as well. I can't close the book on my cowgirl and say, "OK, I've finished all she has to say," because I still have things to say. I'm still changing. The book's not been closed on me yet.*

COWBOY POET
Matador

There's a line in the movie *Urban Cowboy* where Sissy asks Bud, "You a real cowboy?" and Bud answers, "That depends on what you think a real cowboy is." In Texas, that's a legitimate question and, I suppose, a legitimate answer. There are lots of folks who call themselves cowboys. But I'm here to tell you that we know lots of *real* cowboys, and, well, most folks who call themselves cowboys ain't.

Picture what a cowboy should look like and you'll picture Dennis Gaines. But Dennis is not a born-in-the-saddle cattle puncher. Just a few years ago he was working oil rigs in the Gulf of Mexico. Today he is living the legend of a Texas cowboy on the TP City Ranch near Matador, Texas.

Dennis: *I like being outdoors. This is a job to have if you want to be outdoors. It suits some people—the ridin' and being out in the weather testing yourself against the elements.*

But Dennis is doing more than living that life—he's trying to capture its essence in poetry and verse.

A greasy hat with battered crown and brim that curled and bent
and a quart for drinkin' slow and neat
roamed along that barren range with my soul and money spent
and a ticket for my saddle from the pawn shop down the street.
For a puncher's just a fossil in a world that doesn't care
and honors not the virtues of the breed.
Self-reliance, honesty, and treatin' others fair
are just the latest victims of our modern-day stampede.

Dennis: *Some people make it out to be romantic, but there's really nothin' of a romance in it except what a man wants to make of it. Cowboys, cow punchers tend to be some of the world's greatest sentimentalists. They're not always realistic.*

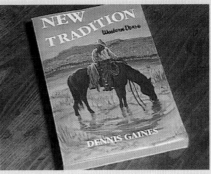

But Dennis found enough romance in his work to start writing down his experiences, hoping to explain the myth and the magic of the cowboy. In his book of western verse, Dennis has found the words to describe the images and emotions of a life few of us will ever understand.

Dennis: *I've written about tradition—how a cowboy feels about religion, moral lessons. And I've written my fair share of cowboy buffoonery, too.*

> I'll give this to Jack
> he rode the galoot at least to the eight-second whistle.
> When his foot chucked out of his hung up boot
> and he sailed like a misguided missile.
> Now folks, I've seen them Chinese acrobats,
> I've seen a bear hit a baseball too,
> but I've never saw nothin' as rare as that
> cause out through there Jack flew.
> With a lazy loop and a spiral spin
> and on like a cannonball
> his scream raised hackles up and down my skin.
> It was a terrible fall.

Dennis: *Sometimes I just feel compelled to put something down because I feel strongly about it, and maybe nobody else in the world would give two figs for it. But it makes me feel good to have it on paper anyway.*

> Jack lived to ride another day,
> then drifted to parts unknown.
> Son, I'll tip my hat to your grand display.
> You're in a class all your own.

Dennis: *If you'd a' told me when I got out of high school—I did get my ABCs through the twelfth grade—that I'd be writin' poetry of any sort sixteen or eighteen years later, I'd a' looked at you like you didn't have any more sense than a stomped duck.*

It should come as no surprise to learn Dennis had never written poetry before. These days finding the time for poetry comes catch-as-catch-can, an hour here, a few minutes there, any time there's a moment's break.

Dennis: *It's not something I sit down and just do easily. It doesn't just come rushing out. I work long hard hours trying to get the verses and the message that I'm trying to say on paper. Matter of fact I think I may spend an inordinate amount of time trying to git my writings the way I want them to sound. It either just doesn't come easily, or it's sometimes maybe a little too complex for my limited brain cells to handle.*

It has been said there are still plenty of cowboys around—you just can't see them from the road. Dennis Gaines looks and rides like a cowboy, and he even writes cowboy poetry, but none of that makes Dennis a cowboy, not yet.

Dennis: *I've got a lot of years left before I'll claim that title for myself. There's a lot of good ol' hands that worked years 'fore they figure they could call themselves an honest-to-God cowboy. I'm just a man who works on a ranch and punches cattle for a livin'.*

> Ranges don't reach to the sunrise
> but the coyote still sings to the dawn
> and the old ways are dying in my eyes.
> How long, Lord, can we carry on?
> Where do you ride now, old cowboy?
> Do the stars in your night brightly shine?
> Do you dream the same dreams I dream now, boy,
> or is your land much grander than mine?
> Does your grass feel the cut of the barbed wire
> that slashes the heart and the hands
> or can it rekindle the old fire
> that sleeps in the soul of this man?

Cowboys, cattle, and land as far as the eye can see. These are the everyday images of life as a cattle puncher. To some it is romantic; for others it's just hard work. Dennis sees it as something very important, something that has to be written down, preserved as poetry that will make you laugh, cry, respect, and maybe understand the life of the cowboy.

Dennis: *Every now and then I'll sit down and write something because I feel like I gotta put it down on paper even if nobody ever gets a chance to read it. But it does bring a little bit of satisfaction if someone reads it and likes it, or if I get to recite for someone and they happen to enjoy it. Yeah, it's a little bonus, a little gravy on the biscuits, so to speak.*

WILLIE DON'T STOP
NO MORE

Luckenbach

hen we rolled through Luckenbach, ten years and a lot of history had passed since "that song" had come and gone. "Let's go to Luckenbach, Texas/With Willie and Waylon and the boys/That distressing life we're living's/Got us feudin' like the Hatfields and McCoys." The big crowds were gone, and by then, that song had become annoying.

Nobody remembers the last time Willie was here. It's not like Luckenbach's been forgotten. The general store is still in business. Folks still drop by. They're lured by the tales that hang around Texas folklore like cobwebs. Stories of Hondo Crouch, a local rancher, buying up this place twenty or so years ago just so he'd have a cold beer handy whenever he wanted one. Stories of Willie Nelson and the rest of his outlaw gang hiding out here, drinking Lone Stars, picking guitars, and generally loafing like regular people. Today, there's still no sign of Willie or

Waylon—or any of the boys for that matter. Hondo is here, memorialized in bronze. Locals still drop by to drink a cold one and tell a few lies. Lydia Hayes has been here since the beginning. She takes care of the place.

> **Lydia:** *No, it's not dying. If you'd been here last weekend or the weekend before, there were several thousand people here at one time. It's not dying. People still come out here and play music, and it's still a neat place to come. And nobody's forgotten about it, that's for sure.*

Things have changed some, though. But for Lydia, the more they change, the more they stay the same. Luckenbach's still Luckenbach.

YOU CAN STILL DROP BY LUCKENBACH FOR SOME CONVERSATION AND A COLD ONE. THAT WILL PROBABLY NEVER CHANGE.

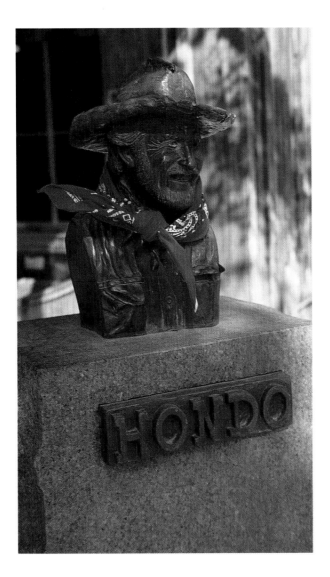

Lydia: *Well, there are not quite as many signs on the side of the building, and the oak trees are a lot bigger. And the speed bump in the middle of the road is there—it wasn't there before. And there are a few things that are missing, and a few things that are added. Not very much though. It's pretty much the same. It's real hard to describe. It's kind of a state of mind.*

Tourists trickle in, look around, carve their names and initials, and move on. Yes, you can still drop by Luckenbach for some conversation and a cold one. That will probably never change.

Lydia: *It's a place to come out, drink a cold beer, sit under the trees, and play or listen to music and just kind of forget about all of the problems in the world. Just have a nice, relaxing time. Makes you feel like you're back in the old days when things weren't quite so complicated.*

It's been more than twenty years now since Willie and Waylon made such a fuss over this speck of a town. Things are pretty quiet now. Luckenbach has returned to its peaceful past. Peaceful, but not forgotten. Stop by, and you probably will not hear that song. But you can still carve your initials in the side of the old store. Lots of people have over the years. Bill and Marla from Lubbock left theirs back in '72. They're still here. Fred from Munich, Germany, his are still here, too. And the Jefferson family from Seattle, Washington. They're all here, right where they put them. Maybe you'd like to drop by too. There are worse ways to pass a lazy Texas afternoon.

SINCE OUR STORY . . .

After 150 years of business, Luckenbach is still there, and it really hasn't changed much. It's still just a tiny Hill Country hamlet with a blacksmith shop, post office, beer joint, dance hall, and cotton gin. It seems someone forgot to tell Luckenbach it's a new century. We couldn't be happier about that!

KING'S COWBOY
Kingsville

t is an empire that claims more brush country than any ranch in Texas. At nearly a million acres, you'd be hard-pressed to find a bigger ranch in the world. They say winter comes to the north side of the King Ranch a full month before it finds its way down to the south forty. There's enough fence here to stretch from Kingsville to Boston, 2,000 miles in all, and Alberto Vio Trevino, known hereabouts as Lolo, has ridden every foot of it.

Lolo was working this ranch long before most of today's hands were born—rounding up cattle by the millions with a good horse, a lot of grit, and a lifetime of saddle sense. But Lolo is slowing down these days.

>**Lolo:** *Well, I have to come here and the first thing I have to do is build a fire, get some water for the coffee, warm up that skillet, and also feed my horse, and then start warming some bread and cut it as soon as possible, you know, so when the visitors come everything is ready.*

Yes, these days the morning fire burns not for branding irons, but for coffee. And an old Ford is a lot easier to saddle up at sunrise.

>**Lolo:** *I never thought I was gonna be driving an LTD. All I knew is about horses and wagons, and now things are a little different.*

Things are different for Lolo. The days are gone for him to ride the range in search of stray calves. These days, Lolo keeps a keen eye out for tourists. A new group arrives about every hour. They come from all over the world, and Lolo loves telling about his world, greeting them, talking about the old days on the ranch, even introducing them to his horse.

>**Lolo:** *How's everybody this morning? Welcome to the King Ranch. Care for a cup, sir? Whenever you're all through, if you don't mind standing somewhere here facing the pens, I'll bring my horse out to introduce him to you all. Come out here! Come on!*

The people are fascinated with Lolo. To them, he's a real cowboy. And he *is* real. It's just that Lolo is from a different time, a different world. He never bothered to get a formal education. Never saw a need for it. From the time he could stand, all he ever wanted out of life was to sit astride a good horse on a well-worn saddle and spend his life as a cowboy.

>**Lolo:** *If I make a mistake, please excuse me. 'Cause I don't hear too good, and I don't speak too good English either.*

For better than sixty years, Lolo has lived that life of a cowboy. And like the ranch he's watched the world from since 1939, Lolo is a south Texas legend. Still, he's reluctant to call himself a true cowboy.

> **Lolo:** *All my life, all I was interested in was riding horses. At first, we used to ride 'em bareback, you know. I'd hesitate to call myself a real cowboy, but I have been with wonderful cowboys, and I have learned from them a little bit.*

It's not surprising that Lolo still misses the cowboy life, but at least staying on the ranch is the next best thing.

> **Lolo:** *I would rather be rounding up cattle or looking for animals that is missing in the pasture. And roping and tying by myself. I think that I can do those things again. I never thought I was gonna be making coffee for visitors. But at least I'm still here on the ranch working. And I'll be here all my life. Every day I see some cowboys working, I wish I was there with them.*

But Lolo's not with them any more. Talking to tourists is what he does.

> **Lolo:** *You all have a nice day. Thank you for your visit. Vaya con dios. So long. Thank you for visiting the King Ranch. So long, sir. Vaya con dios.*

There's an old song that asks, "What do you do with an old cowboy?" Well, you can retire them from the range, but don't ever take them inside. Not when there are still stories left to tell and still folks that'll darn sure come out to listen. It's taken a lot of old cowboys to tame the West and to make the King Ranch the awesome ranching empire it has become. And one of those old cowboys is a humble man known only as Lolo, who never wanted to be anything but a cowboy.

LINK TO A LEGEND

Dublin

ong before the Spanish explorers traveled Texas in search of gold, long before the French attempted to establish their artists' colonies in this enchanted land, long before the fathers of the Republic of Texas declared their independence from Mexico, there was another group of people who called Texas "home." They had no flag, no foreign diplomats; some didn't even have permanent houses. Still, their influence was strong and is still felt today. It was the Native Americans, the people we call "Indians," who were here long before the rest.

After a lifetime of living in what they call the white man's world, Monroe Tahmahkera and his Native American wife, Sandra, now live the Comanche way of life. That doesn't mean living in a teepee or hunting for food. It is a spirit and a belief, a bond with the land and its creatures.

> **Sandra:** *This area is the old Comancheria. This was Comanche land even before any white people came to this area. And even after they started migrating to this area, it still remained Comanche land.*

Monroe grew up with horses, but he didn't sit a saddle 'til the age of twenty-three. Like his Comanche ancestors before him, he rides bareback. On their sixty-one acres, Monroe and Sandra have fifteen head of horses. They breed Appaloosas and sell the colts.

> **Monroe:** *The more you work with a horse, the gentler he gets. The first thing you've got to do is get their attention. And after you get their attention, they depend on you to tell 'em what to do and when to do it.*

Monroe Tahmahkera has never been one to whisper to a horse. But his method of training is just as effective and even more mysterious than the one in the movies. Monroe's technique dates back hundreds of years, because this old cowboy uses the old Indian ways.

Monroe: *You can put the rope on either foot, the right or the left. And the reason for that is whenever you're working cattle and the horse gets his foot tangled up in it, he knows it's not gonna hurt him. It's just the old way that I was taught when I was just a little kid. That's the way the old Indians used to work 'em.*

For Monroe, being a Comanche is more than just a race, color, or creed. Being Native American is a proud tradition and the link to a legend.

Monroe: *Quanah Parker, my great-grandfather, was the last chief of the Comanches.*

Some say he was the embodiment of the American West. The Texas-born son of Indian captive Cynthia Parker and Chief Nocona, Quanah Parker fought for years, defending the rights of his people. When he finally surrendered in 1875, he became the last Comanche to give up the fight. Quanah Parker soon adjusted to so-called civilization, becoming a rancher, preacher, sheriff, and judge. But his most important role remained as leader and spokesman for his tribe, creating for him a place in history and a legacy of greatness.

BEING A COMANCHE IS MORE THAN JUST RACE, COLOR, OR CREED.

Bob: *I've heard people say that Quanah Parker was the great coming together of the American Indians and the white man.*

Monroe: *I believe he was. I honestly believe that because he did such a great job at it, really.*

Sandra: *You know what I would like to say about him? He came from a true Texas love story. And he lived to create one of his own. When you think of him in that manner, there are a lot of people that are in love with him still today. Because he touched so many lives, Indians and non-Indians.*

For Monroe and Sandra, Fossil Rim Wildlife Center in Glenrose, Texas, is a natural setting to demonstrate the American Indian way of life. It's part of their ongoing quest to take their tales across the state and explain what it means to be Native American. School kids love to listen to their tales and watch Monroe's rope tricks.

Sandra: *We try to teach not only about our tribe, but all tribes in general. Just so they can get a little background about Native Americans or Indians in general. Because they're not taught a lot about that in school anymore.*

Bob: *Did you have a tradition that you had to carry on because you are Quanah Parker's great-grandson?*

Monroe: *I don't think I have any that I have to carry. I do it because I want to do it. That's the way I feel about it. Sure he was a great man, but that don't give me any stepping stones or anything of that nature. I think that we make our own trails, and we have to live our own lives, and that's the way I feel about it.*

Bob: *Why have you held on to the old traditions?*

Monroe: *Well, I think that if we don't, it's just like the language. You're gonna lose it. And I think that it's worth my time and other people's time to teach our younger generation about our tribe or other tribes of Indians and their way of living, and I think that if somebody don't do it, it's just gonna be lost.*

The blood of warriors and chiefs runs through his veins. The sorrow and struggles of more than one hundred years are seen in his eyes. He can never forget the suffering of his ancestors like his great grandfather, Quanah Parker, but Monroe looks to a future where all people live in peace. For it is in the shadow of a legend that Monroe Tahmahkera casts his own light for the whole world to see.

A SADDLER'S STORY
San Angelo

sk just about any cowboy out San Angelo way where you can get help for a broken horn or a stitch in a busted stirrup, and any real cowboy worth his salt will tell you to go see Rector. Yep, if you've got a sick saddle or you want a shiny new one, go see Rector Story at the Donaho Saddle Shop.

For more than a century, cowboys and ranchers around these parts have known that a Concho saddle was the best that they could find. And for fifty of those hundred years, Rector Story has been here, patiently and quietly making saddles that have come to be known by riders all over the world as the best saddles anywhere.

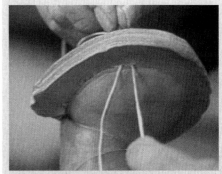

Rector: *Well, they's good as anybody's. They's awfully good saddle makers all over the country too. But we build as good a saddle as anybody else. As best we can. You get a reputation, and everybody, they think, well, they got to have one of 'em. It's just like styles and cars and things like that. If friends got one of 'em, you got to have one of 'em too.*

Concho Street used to be one of the most rootin' tootin', wild and woolly streets in all of Texas, and the Donaho Saddle Shop sat stoically in the middle of it all. Today the shop is situated between two antiques stores. Things aren't like they used to be on Concho Street. But Rector remembers the wild times because he was here. He watched it all from the back of the saddle shop and saw the street change while this little saddle shop stayed the same.

Rector: *When I went to work down here, it was just about as rough as you've ever seen in your life. And you've seen these Wild West shows. They had nothing on Concho Street. Oh, we changed with the times, of course. Now, as far as the way we build a saddle, it hasn't changed much—only how the saddle finishes out. We have to change the styles to stay with the*

trends. We don't make the trends, and we don't make the styles. We just follow them.

Some folks might think there's not much call for a saddle maker anymore. Fact is, Rector has all the business he can handle. Especially when a new saddle is only a phone call away.

Rector: *I have customers come in here, that have phoned in here for years, but that I have never seen before. There's one particular customer from Florida that came in here a few years ago, walked in the front door, and says, "I bet you $100 you don't know who I am." I says, "Well, just save your money, Mr. Peebles, 'cause I know just who you are." He couldn't figure it out, but I'd talked to him so much on the phone that I recognized his voice.*

Back in 1938, when R. E. Donaho gave Rector a job as apprentice, he had no idea he would later sell the place to him. He probably had less of an idea that fifty years later this modest little man would still own the saddle shop and that it would still bear the name of the man who hired him.

Rector: *One time one of the salesmen came through here, and he says, "I'd change that name if I was you." And I said, "No, the name Donaho has been here for a long time, and I'm not gonna change it." And he says, "No, I'd make it Rector's Saddle School." He says that every shop in the state of Texas has somebody that trained here. We've trained most of the saddle makers in Texas.*

More and more these days, factory machines are replacing handmade saddles and self-made men like you'll find at the Donaho Saddle Shop. Rector is one of the last real saddle makers, a trade that takes years to learn and years to teach. It is time the new apprentices aren't willing to spend.

> **Rector:** *The young people, they want to work six months and be the boss. They have these schools, saddle-making schools. The people go in there, and they weld two to three saddles, and they come out, and they're saddle makers in their estimation. To me, they couldn't even repair without help.*

There was a time in this country when the family business was passed down to the younger generation as the years wore on. Since the mid-1800s, Donaho's has been handed down to a saddle maker that learned the trade right here. Could be, though, that Rector is the last of a long line of owners and one of the last true craftsmen of a great art form of the Old West.

> **Bob:** *Who gets it after you?*

> **Rector:** *Well, I have a grandson's going to college out here. He's a big commercial artist. I don't know whether he'll take up the trade or not. I would rather somebody own it that had learned the trade here. He's got to have interest in it to make a go of it, and at the present time his interest is all that commercial art.*

But Rector has never tired of the work, and his interest in it has never flagged.

> **Rector:** *Everything's new. Every saddle you build is different. It's very interesting work. It's the only thing I've ever known.*

SINCE OUR STORY . . .

Donaho Saddle Shop is still open, but Rector Story has retired. The new owner, Jeff Kimball, plans to continue the tradition of making fine custom saddles and tack.

CREATURES GREAT & SMALL

THEIR OWN LITTLE KINGDOM

Murchison

ff the main road near Murchison, Texas, where the edge of the Piney Woods meets the prairie, is a refuge for animals—an oasis where the abused and the mistreated can find a place of rest and be cared for without exploitation. It's a place where they can live out their days doing what they please, a place not unlike the one described in Anna Sewell's novel *Black Beauty*.

At the Black Beauty Ranch a sign inscribed with the last lines of the book reads: "I have nothing to fear, and here my story ends. My troubles all are over and I am at home." Chris Byrne is the shepherd of the mistreated, tending to his flocks' needs and seeing that no more harm will venture their way.

Chris: *It's time to give the animals a break. All the animals on the planet are being exploited one way or the other. Every one of them is in some sort of trouble somewhere.*

At Black Beauty Ranch, they're no longer in trouble.

Chris: *We've got llamas, horses, burros, foxes, pigs, all kinds of animals. We even have a wildlife area, and if somebody has a snake in their backyard, or they find an injured possum, or a hawk that has been shot by somebody, they bring it here. We have an area where we can release them, and we just put them back in the wild.*

Cleveland Amory was the savior of these animals. The profits from his books have gone to feed the starving creatures and to support Black Beauty Ranch through his Fund for Animals.

Cleveland: *A burro is the beast of burden of the entire world, and if there's any animal that was mistreated all over the globe, it probably is the burro. I wanted one place where every single burro would be happy. Almost all these that you see here were rescued, either from the Grand Canyon, from China Lake, the Naval Weapons Center, or from*

Death Valley. All would have been shot. They understand very quickly what's going on, that this is a place where nobody's going to hurt you.

Bob: *What would it do to you personally if you lost all this, and you couldn't take care of all the animals anymore?*

Cleveland: *Well, I don't think it would happen now, thanks to* The Cat Who Came to Christmas. *It's now sold almost two million copies. There's a little put aside, you know. I wouldn't let it go—we owe it to these animals. A lot of them will live out their lives here. I just wanted someday to have a place where there would be no abuse of animals whatsoever and really not any use of them. We don't even ride around here. The animals do what they want.*

A PLACE WHERE THEY CAN LIVE OUT THEIR DAYS DOING AS THEY PLEASE

Animals like Conga, a 10,000-pound African elephant, who once lived in a roadside zoo in Florida.

Chris: *Conga is about nineteen years old. She's from Naples, Florida. She wouldn't train too well, and the people were punishing her. They were hosing her down and putting a lamp cord in the water to shock her, so she came here with a lot of problems. She was very aggressive. She's got lots of room now, and she got her own pool and stuff. She's settled down and she's real nice.*

Bob: *Is there really a need for a place like this?*

Chris: *There's a need for a lot of places like this. You could carve one big chunk of the planet and have it be that kind of place. Let the animals have their own little kingdom and do their own thing.*

Bob: *Why? What's the problem?*

Chris: *I don't think we understand animals enough. They're here for a reason. I think we should take responsibility for our actions and realize they are wiping out the animals. It needs to stop, it needs to slow down. I think somewhere down the line we're gonna realize there's more to animals than we know about right now, a lot more. We are on the planet cohabiting with these other creatures. We don't have a special license to say we are gonna be the only one. I don't think we have that kind of authority. I think there's a bigger plan going on. They have a part in it.*

Chris is the shepherd and Cleveland Amory the savior of more than 500 horses, burros, elephants, chimps, pigs, cats, and just about any other animal you can think of. The creatures have been saved from an almost certain painful death to live out their lives in a place with no fear, a place where their stories can quietly end, where they feel at home—at Black Beauty Ranch.

SINCE OUR STORY . . .

Cleveland Amory, the founder of Black Beauty Ranch and The Fund for Animals, died on October 15, 1998. He is survived by his daughter and granddaughter, a three-legged orange cat, many burros, elephants, horses, chimpanzees, pigs, sheep, deer, goats, monkeys, wolves, buffalo, llamas, bobcats, prairie dogs, pumas, eland, and four kinkajous.

Chris Byrne still manages Black Beauty Ranch.

CALLING ALL PIGS

Bainer Switch

oxanne Ward's found her calling—calling hogs. It's not exactly the kind of talent one makes into a career, but Roxanne's only in it for the fun anyway. She has spent a lifetime in self-proclaimed hog heaven. With her passion for pigs, Roxanne has brought together just about every ceramic swine and porcelain piglet she's ever had the good fortune to find. In fact, around Bainer Switch she's known as the Pig Lady. And Roxanne says that tickles her pig pink.

Roxanne: *I know I probably should be ashamed to be called Pig Lady, but that's really a compliment because there's a difference between a pig and a hog. And it's 160 pounds. So if you're going to call me something, call me a pig, don't call me a hog.*

Trust us, when it comes to hog calling, we'll leave that to Roxanne. She's participated in twenty-eight hog-calling contests and has never been defeated. When it comes to competition, Roxanne Ward knows how to bring home the bacon.

Roxanne: *Soooooeeeeeee pig! Now I hog-call every day. I hog-call my potbellied pig named Oscar. Oscar is the most precious little pig that I've ever owned.*

Roxanne doesn't just confine her hog calling to the hollers around Bainer Switch. She can be quite a ham. If there's an audience around, Roxanne can be found right up front. She's a hit on the tube and a champion on the circuit.

Roxanne: *Every time that I would hear of a hog-calling contest, I would compete, and I'd win, and I'm still winning contests. Still having a hog-wild time. I'm real easy to please. Just give me a pig and a Diet Coke, and I'll follow you anywhere.*

"JUST GIVE ME A PIG AND A DIET COKE, AND I'LL FOLLOW YOU ANYWHERE."

Roxanne doesn't attribute all of her success to skill. It all has to do with superstition, good luck, and a good uniform.

Roxanne: *When I hog-call, I always wear my sunflower hat, and I wear a bow on my toe for good luck. I can't hog-call without it. I take it serious, but you have to have fun with it. I'm glad I have a chance to make people happy and make 'em smile with my hog calling. And I feel this is what hog heaven is like. That's just what I think it would be.*

SINCE OUR STORY . . .

Roxanne Ward is still callin' the hogs, big and small. She's won several more hog-calling contests and she still wears her good-luck outfit each and every time she calls—wouldn't think of doing it without that bow on her toe. She's also added a new superstition to her calling routine; she always removes her shoes before calling the hogs.

Roxanne is a regular guest at our Texas Country Reporter Festival held every fall.

BUTTERFLY RANCH

Swinney Switch

I n Swinney Switch, Texas, livestock way outnumber the people, cows, pigs, horses, and goats. Roundup time is a busy time in these parts, but at the Homeyer Ranch you'd be hard-pressed to find even one cowboy during roundup time. There's not much riding, roping, or branding done. No fences to mend or horses to shoe. Bethany Homeyer can round up the entire herd without breaking a sweat. She runs the biggest ranch in Texas for butterflies.

Bethany: *We had cattle, now we have caterpillars—from cattle to caterpillars. When we were in the cattle business, we'd mainly have our roundups spring and fall, and now that I'm in the butterfly business, it's basically a roundup everyday. Most people just look at them as worms. They're not just worms, they're my puppies.*

Bethany's always been a country girl. Waterfowl, wildlife, and livestock have always been right off her own back porch.

Bethany: *I like to come out here in the mornings and look across the lake. Many times we'll see a deer going down to the water. Or the does with their fawns. There's so much wildlife just in this little backyard.*

But it's the delicacy and beauty of butterflies, the personality of caterpillars, that inspire her life calling.

Bethany: *They're probably one of the most beautiful creatures ever created. Each of these little guys have their own personality. Sometimes they're not always willing just to start feeding. So what I do is unfurl the proboscis, which is just like a little straw, and help 'em, and then there he goes. We don't raise them for wool. We don't raise them for anything other than to be set free, free to fly. When I package my butterflies, they've already been hand-fed and exercised.*

This is no fly-by-night operation. You could call it the King Ranch of Butterflies. Bethany's butterflies are shipped all over the country.

Bethany: *Those are going to New Hampshire. There's some going to Arizona, Illinois, Indiana. We have a funeral that we're delivering to, a wedding, and a memorial. It's amazing that something so simple can bring so much pleasure. It keeps me going when I get letters from people telling me how the butterflies have touched their lives, helping them to heal or to understand the tragedy in their life. That's the most important thing about all of this.*

"IT'S AMAZING THAT SOMETHING SO SIMPLE CAN BRING SO MUCH PLEASURE."

Like all endings and beginnings, there is a tender story behind Bethany's butterfly ranch. After losing her son Michael, in despair she looked everywhere for hope and found it in only one place: outside her kitchen window in the leaping, swooping flits and dives of the butterfly.

Bethany: *To hold them, to feel them, their little butterfly kisses—it's not just a butterfly, they're not little bugs back there. I truly believe that they were put on this earth to heal. And I didn't realize that until I found out how many lives they do touch. These butterflies truly help to heal those that hurt.*

Delicate and elegant, their silent beauty comes, then is gone so quickly. Bethany Homeyer's house turned butterfly barn is no longer an empty place. The sadness of a loss has been replaced with the hopeful fluttering of tiny wings, dances in midair, that celebrate hope and healing even in the worst of times.

Bethany: *The butterfly is symbolic of the same hope that we have of new life, a new beginning. We are here for a moment, and then we're gone, no matter how long our lifetime is. The butterfly is here for a moment, and he flits off, and he's gone.*

HOG HEAVEN
Boerne

hey are the cast-off companions, casualties of a passing fad, rejected when they outgrew the yard. But although their owners may have dumped them and never looked back, pigs of all kinds have found a home with Angharad Rees at Safe Harbor Refuge.

Angharad: *Right now, we're about seventy pigs. Mostly we have potbellied pigs. We have anywhere from the miniatures to the standards. Standard potbellied pigs get to be about 250, 300 pounds. Miniatures stay about 30 to 50 pounds. And then we have mixtures of domestic pigs along with potbellies.*

The spelling of her name's a little tricky, but the definition is divine. It's an old Celtic word meaning "safe harbor." And for a special breed of animals, it's the safest place they've known.

Angharad: *Back in the seventies, when potbellied pigs were introduced from out of the United States, the rage caught on. Everybody wanted to have one. But they don't get cute as they get older. And most people were told that pigs will stay small, but they usu-*

118

ally top out at 300 pounds. And pigs can live about ten to fifteen years. People get tired of them, and either ignore them or turn them loose, thinking they can take care of themselves. Or, hopefully, they call someone like us and we try to give them some comfort.

To see her riding around the ranch on her tractor, you'd never guess Angharad works as a hospice nurse. Running a pig refuge is another full-time job. And without a paid staff or volunteers, it's up to Angharad and her family to get the chores done.

Angharad: *We have a 1953 Farmall tractor. We call her the tomboy. She's as old as me and looks as good as me. Our treat is to load her up with the food and take her down to the lower compound and feed the animals. We don't feed slop to our pigs. We don't give 'em meat products because that's what causes most pig areas to smell. People say pigs stink. That's a fallacy. The only time they'll smell is if they're given meat by-products or grease. These guys just get fruits and vegetables and grain products.*

"PEOPLE SAY PIGS STINK. THAT'S A FALLACY."

Porkers can make real pigs of themselves, and the cost of feeding so many gets higher every day. Angharad does get a few donations, and a neighboring restaurant saves scraps. But most of the money comes out of her own pocket. And on a nonprofit pig farm, times get lean.

Angharad: *When we started getting all these pigs, we were really getting scared. We don't want to turn a pig away. It would just break my heart if we had to turn any pig*

*away. We have to put a lot of things to the side. Our house is unfinished. I don't think
I've bought new clothes in the last two years. You figure those things are not as important as providing for the animals that really need to be saved and to be taken care of for
the rest of their lives.*

Angharad's work doesn't end at the refuge gate. She travels all over to places
like the Lions Camp in Kerrville, spreading animal awareness and getting kids
up close and personal with pigs.

Angharad: *We're reading pig stories to the Lions camp this year, to the children, and
teaching them about what it really means to take care of a pet. What the responsibility
is, what the rewards are.*

Unfortunately, the message against cruelty comes far too late for many of Angharad's little guys. She not only takes in unwanted potbellies, she also rescues
them, saving them from lives of neglect and outright abuse.

Angharad: *This one's missing her right ear completely. We were told that dogs had gotten hold of her and completely ripped the ear off. A lot of people say that animals don't
have souls. Well, I disagree with that. When you love an animal, when you make it a
pet, I think you awaken its soul, and they learn to love, they learn to show fear. And
they learn to show affection. When you awaken an animal's soul, I think the worst thing
you can do to it is ignore it or abandon it or take it to the meat market. They have personalities just like humans do. They want to be loved, they want to give love, and they
deserve the same respect that we would expect for ourselves.*

IN SEARCH OF A SYMBOL

Burnett

It's the first week in November and it's eagle time on the Colorado River. American bald eagles spend their winter here, and we're in search of them, and a lot more, on what's called a "Vanishing Texas River Cruise."

Richard Cook, our guide, knows this river like most of us know the freeway home. He lives on the Colorado and works on the river cruise, pointing out the special beauty to those who may need a leg up in getting back to basics.

> **Richard:** *Once again, I'd like to welcome everybody to the Vanishing Texas River Cruise. It's gonna be about a 25-mile round-trip, 2½ to 3 hours long. As we head up the Texas Colorado, I'll be pointing out the wildlife, the wildflowers, and the scenic area along the way.*

We're traveling the Colorado on the northern edge of Lake Buchanan, an area that looks today like it must have looked centuries ago. Our vessel is named the *Eagle Two*, a boat built specially for cruising these waters. The hundred or more passengers are people from the big city mostly. They search the shore anxiously for any sign of wildlife, looking for reassurance, for proof that the world isn't all made of concrete and steel.

> **Richard:** *It's a very undeveloped area, wilderness area, but it's not publicly owned. It's privately owned. But the water is publicly owned, it's owned by the state, so you can have access to all this beautiful country only by water. There's no access by land. And in large measure, that's why this area has stayed as pristine as it has.*

It's an Ansel Adams photograph, a Thomas Cole painting of scenes they thought disappeared with the arrival of skyscrapers and satellite dishes. But the Colorado is still here and so are its scenic shores and animal life you'd be hard-pressed to find anywhere else this close to civilization.

Richard: *For us that live here, we take this all for granted. We see it day in and day out. We forget what it's like to live in a big city where you live in an apartment, and you have to fight traffic. It's beautiful country here. You have waterfalls, you have abundant wildlife and things that most people don't see day in and day out.*

What you don't see day in and day out in the city is nature untouched, the wondrous sights and sounds of wilderness. What these people came here to see, though, is even more magnificent than all this. They came to see the American bald eagle in its winter nesting grounds on the Colorado. Richard Cook knows everything else on the cruise is a warm-up for that magical moment when one of the great birds decides to make an appearance.

Tourist 1: *That's what you call King of the Mountain.*

Tourist 2: *That was a real thrill. I've never seen one, and boy, just to see it that soon and right by the water and all. I love it!*

Richard: *Even the staff members—we see 'em day in and day out—we never get tired of 'em. It's almost like going to church.*

For some, it's a celebration; for others, an emotional experience. The river, the wildlife, the feeling that all is right because this is still here. It's a symbol of something we want so desperately to continue, a part of us we refuse to let go, no matter how high-tech our world becomes.

Richard: *We've seen men cry on this cruise. It happens all the time. It's a very moving experience. Because, unless you've gone to Alaska where they have thousands of them, seeing one is going to be a very moving experience, because we're all patriots. We may not think we are, but we are.*

Back in the early seventies when we first started traveling around the state, there were only about 3,000 bald eagles left in the country. Today, there are more than 20,000, and about 500 of those birds choose Texas as their winter nesting ground.

Richard: *We're in one of the fastest growing states in the Union and one of the fastest growing regions of country. And as Austin grows, this area is going to develop more. You're going to have more houses, and this slice of Texas, which is the Texas that they saw 150 years ago when they settled this area, is going to slowly disappear.*

Yes, this picturesque setting may only be here for a short time longer. After all, this is the Vanishing Texas River Cruise.

SINCE OUR STORY . . .

Richard Cook left Vanishing Texas River Cruise many years ago, but the original owners are still operating daily trips. You can find it just off Ranch Road 2341 on the east side of Lake Buchanan. We've taken this cruise at least thirty times and find each trip to be more interesting than the previous.

WHOOPERS ON THE FRONT LINE

Rockport

Take a trip aboard the *M. V. Skimmer* with Captain Ted Appell in the coastal waterways near Rockport, and you'll see firsthand how nature works. You'll see Captain Ted's world, a fragile place where beauty and the future hang in the balance.

Ted: *Folks, we're going to head out across Aransas Bay and not only visit the beautiful rookery islands here on the Texas coast, but also the rare, endangered whooping crane.*

"There are men too gentle to live among wolves," James Cavanaugh wrote. When he returned home from Vietnam, Ted Appell realized he is such a man. So he decided to live among the peaceful creatures found along Texas' intercoastal waterways.

Ted: *We'll stop up for a minute or two on this little island. I want you to look at the vegetation that's on this island. This is all salt water out here. This is not fresh water. We have some wild snapdragons growing out here, and wolfberry bushes.*

Captain Ted Appell is a gentle man, a man who chooses to live his life among gentle creatures, like the white egret he points out on the "beautiful virgin-type beach."

Ted: *A gentleman the other day asked, "Captain, what's your description of a virgin beach?" And I didn't know the answer real quick, so I just said, "One that doesn't have a damn condominium on it." I am a conservationist. This whole area and all our estuaries are extremely important. Everything that lives in the ocean depends on these estuaries for food or breeding.*

Ted has always had a love of wildlife. The tours enable him to educate others, to help people understand the importance of the Texas coast and the marsh areas. It's his way of contributing.

Ted: *This would make an excellent rookery island. The only problem is that the reefs make it easily accessible to the coyotes and coons. You got one snowy egret moving* *around there. Several reddish egrets. Isn't that beautiful? Look at that! OK, we're in the coastal waterways, and we're coming down through the heart of the Aransas Wildlife Refuge. We'll be watching on the right-hand side for our whooping cranes.*

The pride and joy of Captain Ted's tour is the whooping crane. He feels personally responsible for their safety, for their very existence. He knows every bird and counts their numbers daily.

Ted: *Twenty-one whooping cranes is our count today. Twenty-nine yesterday. The whooping crane is the tallest North American bird, reaching a full-extended height of almost 5-feet—7-to-7½-foot wing span. Body weight runs around eighteen to twenty-two pounds. This is a very impressive bird.*

Take a ride with Captain Ted Appell, and you'll meet a man who chooses to take responsibility for all the gentle creatures in his world, and, he tells us, we must take responsibility too.

Ted: *Every American should be responsible. Each of us has a responsibility to protect this area, because the wildlife is the front line for all of us. This is what I try to teach the people with me on my boat. A lot of people say, "What's so important about a whooping crane?" or "What's so important about ducks?" If they can't hunt it, it's not important. That's wrong.*

If we don't take responsibility, he warns, one day we may pay the price—like we did with the brown pelicans.

Ted: *The brown pelicans taught us DDT was a poison. It killed the brown pelicans, almost demolished 'em on the Texas coast. That's our front line. If it hadn't been for those brown pelicans, we might have been next.*

ROADSIDE TEXAS

VELVET ELVIS

El Paso

Hidden away in an El Paso warehouse is one of the world's largest collections of art. But it's not exactly something that the chamber of commerce prints up on brochures. This is not a metropolitan museum. But it is the source for one of the biggest and gaudiest pop art crazes in America.

Doyle Hardin just may be the most misunderstood man in the art world.

Doyle: *A work of art is only as valuable as what somebody is willing to pay. What do you consider art? To me, if I like it, it's art. This is one of the very popular pieces today. It's the eagle carrying the war bonnet to the Indian spirits in the cloud. This is where the action is now. Indians . . . the vanishing buffalo . . . the white buffalo is a very good item.*

Doyle is not exactly an art aficionado. He's not a collector of Picasso or van Gogh. Doyle's not even big on canvas. He's a velvet man. Black velvet and bright colors. Proof positive that one man's trash is another man's treasure.

Doyle: *The velvet industry began in the early sixties quite by accident. The first purchase I made was simply to supply some stores that I had in Columbus, Georgia. Later on I sold the stores and came west. The velvet has since gone around the world. We've sold them into many foreign countries during the thirty years I've been in the business. I've sold over $100 million worth of velvet paintings.*

Make no mistake. This is big business. At times Doyle's warehouse handles 400,000 to 500,000 paintings in a day. That's a lot of Velvet Elvis, and, of course, there's the rest of the regulars captured in oil-based color: Martin Luther King, John Wayne, John Lennon—even Jesus. Like it or not, black velvet has made a mark on the art world.

Doyle: *You don't find many people that would ever admit to having one in their home. Most people turn thumbs down on the velvets. But they keep selling. The market is as strong today as it was twenty years ago. The vivid bright colors, the simplicity of the art—you don't have to stand on your head or sideways to wonder what these subjects are.*

Where does Doyle get such a bounty of black velvet? Just across the border in Juarez. Local artists turn out paintings at a fast and furious pace, and Doyle's scouts cruise every alley in Juarez in search of the paintings the world seems to have an undying thirst for. It's Doyle's chance to make a dent, or maybe a smear, on the American culture.

HE'S A VELVET MAN. BLACK VELVET AND BRIGHT COLORS.

Doyle: *The velvet originated in Juarez, Mexico, and it still is the capital of the velvet world today. We ship all throughout Mexico, Central America, as well as throughout the United States, Canada, the European market, Australia, New Zealand, Germany—all over—and it all comes from this local area of El Paso and Juarez.*

This booming market doesn't just happen. There's a method behind the madness for these black-and-bright creations.

Doyle: *We use very strong colors. We try to use a certain amount of details but simple enough so that the artist can produce at least one every two hours and keep the cost down within a range that everyone and anyone can afford. We use the finest crates of oil that money can buy. If it gets rained on, it doesn't harm the velvet. In fact, when one gets dusty or dirty, just take a water hose and wash it. It won't harm the painting. We're working into the third generations of artists today—their fathers worked for us, their grandparents worked for us. You have to be talented to some degree.*

Like with all kinds of art, subjects and tastes change—about every three to five years, Doyle Hardin says. Used to be the unicorn. Before that it was outdoor scenes, waterfalls, mountains. What doesn't change is that people want them.

Doyle: *Many times people will come into an art show and they'll make fun, they'll make jokes. "Oh, I gotta have the Velvet Elvis." But they buy Elvis. They buy other works, too.*

I suppose black velvet will always be the black sheep of the art world. There probably won't be any Velvet Elvis Galleries opening soon. But then Doyle Hardin plans to change the way we look at the bright colors on black. He wants to open a museum for the paintings and bring some respect to a definite art form. And who couldn't show a little respect to a painting you can wash off with a hose?

Doyle: *I think I have sold enough velvet paintings to go in every home in the United States. Every wall should be covered, and yet we still sell 'em. They will never go away.*

SINCE OUR STORY . . .

The black velvet paintings seem to be even more popular today than they were when we first ran across this story. The Elvis paintings can no longer be legally produced, which has given the existing paintings "collectors' items" status!

TRAVELING EXHIBIT

Houston

I can't tell you how often we'll be on our way somewhere when suddenly we're sidetracked by something we never expected. There we are, headed down the highway on our way to a story, talking about what we'll do when we get there, when another story jumps right out into the middle of the road and bites us. When that happens, there's nothing we can do but bite back. It happened in Houston. We were driving down the street, quite content with our direction, when it appeared in front of us: The Art Car Museum.

It looks more like a piece of sculpture itself than a gallery. Then again, Brian Taylor will tell you this isn't your average art museum. You won't find paintings on canvas or sculptures of bronze within its walls.

Brian: *We have a lot of interesting and unusual exhibits here. We decided we needed a pretty unique structure to house these type of exhibits.*

The art displayed at The Art Car Museum is all created in the medium of automobile.

Brian: *This is the only art car museum in the world. Houston is the art car capital of the world, and it was decided that if there was going to be an art car museum, it had to be in Houston. I myself work at The Art Car Museum. This is my day job. A lot of my friends are a little jealous. There's just not a lot of cool art car jobs out there. It is strange, and it is weird, and it is bizarre, but it's still fun.*

From buttons to buffalo and baubles to bunnies, if it can be bought up, welded, or glued down, you can bet it's found its home on an art car.

Brian: *My favorite car in the museum has got to be Rex the Rabbit. Its appeal is immediate. It's bigger than life, and Rex is so over the top with his basket of eggs.*

129

When you get down to the nuts and bolts of all this art, this garage-turned-gallery isn't only about art after all. Brian Taylor says there's a lot more to it, and it all starts with . . .

> **Brian:** *Fun. I like fun, and art cars are fun. You cannot drive an art car without it changing your complete driving experience. There's a magic that comes when you regularly drive your art car. It does change your life to a point that once you do one art car, there's probably going to be another art car in your future. And that keeps going until you basically don't have any normal cars in your family anymore.*

"IT IS STRANGE, AND IT IS WEIRD, AND IT IS BIZARRE, BUT IT'S STILL FUN."

Brian Taylor says it's more than just a job being curator of the art cars. It's a lifestyle. After all, art has no boundaries, and with a full tank of gas, these creations give a whole new meaning to "traveling exhibit."

> **Brian:** *You're not expecting any money in return for it. You're not doing it to be shown in a museum. It's basically an incorruptible type of art. It's your basic expression from you to the people on the roads. Whatever's special to you is what you are going to put on your car. Those make the best ones.*

PANCAKES, TEXAS-SIZE

Sterling City

Folks in Sterling City have been waking up to the same aroma every morning for six decades—the smell of bacon frying and coffee brewing down at the City Cafe. Wesley and Joy Turner took over the place years ago. And it's been nonstop eggs over easy ever since. That is, until one day an accident in the kitchen spilled batter into a hubcap-sized hotcake. Breakfast in Sterling City has never been the same.

Wesley Turner gets up early each and every morning. He says he likes it that way.

Wesley: *Morning is my favorite time of the day because it's real quiet, it's calm. But that usually does not last long around here. We open at six o'clock in the morning—six-oh-five, if I sleep in. My wife runs the front. That's her territory, and the back is my territory. The cafe's been here since the thirties.*

Joy: *Do you all want to share the pancake?—because they're huge.*

Wesley: *I've had these things called anything from saddle blankets to hubcaps. Somebody called 'em barrel lids the other day. I guarantee two things about these things. You're gonna get full, and you're gonna remember where you got 'em.*

Customer: *There ain't no way I can eat all of that! She told me they were big, but I didn't think it would be that big. I'm glad I didn't order three.*

Granny: *These crazy people come in here and order two or three pancakes, and you just have to tell 'em that they won't be able to eat that much.*

Bob: *Has anyone ever been able to eat that much?*

Joy: *A 10-year-old boy and a 90-year-old woman.*

Bob: *A 90-year-old woman? And a 10-year-old boy?*

131

Joy: *Both ate three pancakes apiece. Ninety. Little bitty small petite woman. She finished three pancakes and walked out of here.*

Customer: *I can't eat that whole cake. It's too big. I'll take the other half home and have it for a midmorning lunch.*

Wesley: *There's one drawback to this. I have a very small grill, and I can't hardly cook more than three of these at a time.*

"I GUARANTEE . . . YOU'RE GONNA GET FULL, AND YOU'RE GONNA REMEMBER WHERE YOU GOT 'EM."

Wesley Turner's appetite for the absurd has become the Sterling City challenge. If you can eat a stack of three, the Turners will foot the bill and help wheel you out the door. Of course, that's not such a big prize, since these manhole covers slathered with syrup will set you back just $1.50 apiece.

Joy: *We have old people that come from Lubbock, Odessa, Midland, all over. They'll have one pancake, and they'll split it between them. There's usually pancake left over when they're finished. And they're just tickled to death that they get out of here so cheap.*

Wesley: *It's been a long time since anybody's been able to eat three pancakes. I've had 300-pound guys come in here and order three pancakes. You don't have to worry about these big guys. It's these little skinny guys that come in and say they can eat three. That's when I'll probably have to buy three pancakes for 'em.*

Joy: *Some of 'em come in with this attitude. They say they want three pancakes. And I tell 'em that these pancakes are this big, and you can't eat three of 'em. They say, "Well, I know what I want—just bring it to me anyway."*

Wesley: *I've had a couple of people actually get mad. A couple ordered two pancakes, short stack, and the waitress told 'em. Said, "Look, the things are this big, they are this big. Are you sure you want 'em?" "Yes, I want 'em." She takes 'em out, and the guy says, "You didn't say they were that big." She did say they were that big. They just couldn't believe it. It really is funny.*

Joy: *The older people that live on fixed incomes and Social Security and stuff, like Granny, they depend on places like this.*

Wesley: *Phooey on the all-power dollar. It's silly. The world's crazy about that. Everybody wants to get rich, everybody wants to make money. I'm not that interested in that. I'm looking at the big picture, and I'm trying to do some good for some people around here.*

Several years back, the Turners turned their back on big profits for big pancakes—the buck-fifty stomach-stuffers that'll feed you for a week. What may have been a peculiar pancake blunder seems to have put City Cafe on the map. Which explains that West Texas word of warning: When passing through Sterling City, better loosen your belt and bring a doggie bag for a foot-wide flapjack you just can't get anywhere else.

Wesley: *It's worth it. I enjoy doing it. I want people to be happy when they leave here. I want 'em to remember me. Maybe that's the deal, I want to be remembered for doing the best job I could.*

LEGACY OF LIDS
San Antonio

Barney Smith remembers the days of having to grab the kerosene lantern and Sears catalogue and head outside right in the middle of a Texas blue norther. It was just a part of life. But pipes, pliers, and plumbers changed all that. And when Barney was only knee-high to a monkey wrench, he started sticking his head under people's sinks. Now after a lifetime of plumbing practice and a warehouse of memories, Barney Smith's legacy is a lifetime of lids.

One thing for sure: Barney Smith knows a thing or two about toilets.

Barney: *I've been a plumber for seventy-five years. They say, "You don't look that old." I say, "No, I'm not. But I was born on a plumbing truck." My dad was a master plumber. Lots of patience, and a lot of good common sense is what you have to have in order to get the job done. But most of all, we've got to have a sense of humor.*

Old Barn's got a sense of humor, and a barn in the back of his house. It's a warehouse of sorts.

Barney: *I call this my toilet seat art museum. No telling how many thousands of seats that I've taken out in my lifetime.*

A plumber's shop plum full of toilet seats. Barney Smith has decorated, dedicated, and almost detonated more than 300 lids in his lifetime. And generously hung them out for the world to look at.

Barney: *You're sticking with your profession, and, since I can get these for nothing, you can't beat that. Some of the things that I played with when I was just a small boy growing up in my dad's plumbing shop, I mounted on a toilet seat lid. And none of them you*

don't want to sit on. Open slowly, do not disturb. There are some people who ask me if I've lost my marbles. I say, "No, I haven't lost them—I've got them on a toilet seat."

Of course, he's got all his marbles. And just about every knife, fork, and spoon that's been washed down any drain in south Texas.

Barney: *I have removed ridiculous objects that have been dropped down in the sink drain. Toothbrushes, sucker sticks, even contact lenses. I've removed toys that children have been using in the bathtub—they'd go down into the trap. I believe I've seen it all. I was at Randolph Air Force Base, and I told one of the officers out there that I wanted one of the patches off of his uniform, and he just pulled it off.*

IN TODAY'S WORLD, ONE MAN'S TOILET SEAT IS ANOTHER MAN'S TREASURE.

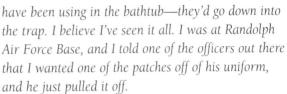

Now it's on a toilet seat. Bashful, Barney's not. This plumbing pack rat would ask for the shirt off your back if it would fit on a toilet seat. Barney will settle for any commode keepsake, long as you'll let him display it in the museum.

Barney: *Whenever I am on a trip, I say "Would you mind me taking this back to put on display?" And they'll say, "Why sure." It doesn't bother me at all to ask for something to put in my museum.*

Folks come from all over to visit Barney's museum—France, Japan, England, Germany. He's got twenty-one countries and 344 signatures listed in the guest book he asks visitors to sign. And that's his second one.

Barney: *Whenever they come through here—they can be going thirty miles an hour down this road— they will turn around and come back and stop. And I say, "Come on in. You got time, I'll show you around. Spend an hour in here, thirty minutes, sign my guest book."*

Barney Smith's gonna have to build a bigger barn for his toilet seat Smithsonian someday. It just proves that, in today's world, one man's toilet seat is another man's treasure.

Barney: *I hate for the telephone to ring and have one of my friends have trouble with their plumbing. I say, "Don't answer the telephone. Let it ring off of the wall." I'd rather work on a toilet seat lid.*

TEXAS, DOWN UNDER

Boerne

exans have always been resourceful, making do with what they have. Well, down in Boerne, Texas, there's a man who's making his living selling a hole in the ground. Eugene Ebell owns a cave right under his front yard. He says it's called the Cave Without a Name. You can drop by most any time and get a personal tour.

To visit the Cave Without a Name, you follow Eugene down a dim stairway, down the hole in his front yard.

> **Eugene:** *Now you can straighten up. We are 94 feet below the ground here. Temperature is 66 degrees all the time. Cool in summer, warm in winter.*

Down here in the cool, damp darkness, 90 feet under another sweltering Texas afternoon, Eugene's got stalagmites, stalactites, and even an underground river. He's got one of the biggest caves in the Texas Hill Country.

> **Eugene:** *I've had all kinds of geologists and college professors down here. I ask them why this cave is so big, and they just sit here and shake their head. They don't know either. We got a whole bunch of formations that look like faces and stuff. You've got to use your imagination down here.*

Eugene never tires of visiting his cave, or of talking about it.

> **Eugene:** *In the beginning, a lot of water came through and picked up dark brown iron oxide mud impurities. So you got the dark colors. Then it settled to a nice orange color, then to a yellow color, and here lately we just got this pure white. Here lately, I mean the last 10,000 years. I've been down here 27,000 times. I still find something new once in a while.*

For more than twenty years Eugene has been taking people for walks through the cave under his front yard. He'll tell you he doesn't need fancy commercials or an amusement park up top to bring folks in. His cave speaks for itself. Even without a name.

Eugene: *We got everything down here. We don't need a lot of ballyhoo. And you see things that you have never seen before. It took 200 million years for some of these things to form. It is real slow in forming. You go on trips, you want to see Paris, Rome, or London, Big Ben, or something. Why not come down here and see these things?*

Bob: *This is part of Texas?*

Eugene: *Oh yeah, definitely. We are right in the middle of it. Underground. This is what you call deep in the heart of Texas!*

SINCE OUR STORY . . .

We first ran this story in 1989, and Eugene Ebell
has since passed away, but daily visits to his cave
are still offered.

PUMPJACK PAINTER

Luling

he city-limits sign reads LULING, but folks around here just call it Oil City. Back in the Roaring Twenties, when Luling was in her heyday and millionaires were made on fifty cents a barrel, this little town produced more than a thousand wells pumping black gold from every spare patch of land. But for every boom, there's a bust, and it hit Luling hard. Today many of the old pumps, called pumpjacks in oil country, are out of work, yet they're still standing as silent reminders of the way things used to be.

George Kalisek is an artist. His home is in Molton, Texas, where he makes signs, banners, and what's called yard art. That is, he did, until he heard about Luling and its plight with the pumpjacks.

> **George:** *I'm a cross between a sign painter and an artist, so I could think of myself as maybe a jack-of-all-trades when it comes to creative things. A pumpjack-of-all-trades, that is.*

Prettying up pumpjacks is no easy job, but while some artists might think this commission too crude, George Kalisek found inspiration in the oil patch. He knew right away that all the pumps needed was identity, personality, and a character of their own.

> **George:** *The rocking motion of the pumpjack will resemble that of a bucking bronc. They asked me to come up with several ideas. Well, you have to stop and think—something that would be appropriate for the motion of the pumpjacks, the way they move back and forth. There's a little bit of science and a little bit of art involved in this job. Plus a little bit of luck.*

He considered a rodeo scene with a "ride 'em cowboy" theme. But George's cowboy will have to stay in the bunkhouse for now. George is in his workshop in Molton, getting another of his characters ready for final construction. He carefully loads each piece from his gigantic jigsaw puzzle and packs them in safely for the trip to their new home. It's a sight to behold. George's old pickup and a behemoth beagle in the bed. The three of 'em travel over dirt roads and highways, through countrysides and town squares, until they finally arrive in Luling, and the real work begins.

> **George:** *This work is hot and very dirty. Especially when you're working with a greasy oil pump. Basically, it's the climbing and the odd angles you have to reach. Other than that, it's a picnic.*

Mounting the character is the hardest part of the job. But in spite of the heat, George's buddy, Junior, is happy to help. In fact, for this project, local folks are ready and willing to pitch in to carry on a tradition started years ago.

> **George:** *They're scattered in all parts of the town—in fields, along the railroad tracks, in the middle of a parking lot, on the school yards, in front yards of business places, wherever you look. And on that pump is some sort of character, which is kind of a treat.*

"IT'S NOT SOMETHING YOU ANALYZE. YOU JUST LOOK AT IT AND ENJOY IT."

Luling has been known for its unique pumpjack creations since George was barely old enough to pick up a paintbrush. But since the old characters have faded or just grown out of date, George is here to replace them with his own original roughneck works of art.

> **George:** *As we go along, we'll probably make more and more intricate designs with more movable parts and more animation. People coming through Luling, the one thing they remember is seeing the pumpjacks decorated as butterflies and as watermelons. The ones we're putting up now, hopefully, will be a new fresh look for them to enjoy.*

George will be the first to tell you that his work may be entertaining, whimsical, or even highly amusing, but it's not for the ages. You just can't do Picasso on a pumpjack.

> **George:** *It's not something you analyze. It's not something you have to find the meaning of. You just look at it and enjoy it.*

You won't find George Kalisek's work at some fancy museum. This is his gallery: the San Marcos Highway intersection with Route 183. And George and the folks in Luling wouldn't have it any other way. Because, just like old Burma Shave signs and old roadside court motels, these painted pump characters are a bit of Americana with a timeless, heartfelt appeal to generations of Texas travelers.

> **George:** *They are landmarks. Some have been here for many years and will continue to be—as long as the oil flows.*

HIDDEN CANYON

Lajitas

I t doesn't take much to imagine outlaws and lawmen facing off in front of the old hotel in downtown Lajitas. It's the kind of place that looks like it never got a face-lift after the Wild West wasn't wild anymore. But we did not come to Lajitas to relive the dusty days of yesteryear. We came here to face the mighty Rio Grande. We came here to go on an adventure, and the adventure we had in mind was far-flung.

Michael Davidson is the founder of Far Flung Adventures. He's been taking people on boat trips down the Rio Grande for about twenty years now. We went along on a daylong, 19-mile trip to experience the almost hidden part of Texas—a magical, majestic place called Santa Elena Canyon.

> **Michael:** *This is pretty rugged country. This portion of the Rio Grande in southwest Texas is more noteworthy for its spectacular scenery and its wild wilderness character than for exciting white water.*

Casually floating downstream from Lajitas, it takes the better part of a day just to get to the canyon, but there's plenty to see along the way.

> **Michael:** *We have a variety of small mammals such as skunks, ring-tail cats, raccoons, badgers. There's the occasional beaver in the river. There are frequent mountain lion and black bear sightings in the national park. We've actually sighted black bear a couple of times along this stretch of river.*

Like an old friend awaiting our arrival, suddenly the canyon appears—an enormous tranquil chasm where the vertical walls are silent sentinels of the ages. Time is at a standstill here, but even the sunlight seems to breathe with life. It's one of those wild, untamed, special places where you feel honored that nature allows you just to be here. It's a place that's awesome in its magnitude, and beautiful beyond belief.

Michael: *What really strikes me, when you look around at the canyon walls and the eons of time this represents, and then look back at the other boat, you realize how insignificant the people are.*

LIKE AN OLD FRIEND AWAITING OUR ARRIVAL, SUDDENLY THE CANYON APPEARS . . .

It's easy to forget this is Texas, but it is. It's one of those special places that have remained hidden from time and development. This is the mythical Texas with its grand vistas and breathtaking views. This is the Texas that only a handful of people get to see.

Michael: *It's not the Texas that most Texans think of, because most of them are from a flatter area, but if you go out into the world, then this is the Texas that people think of.*

Typically Texas or not, Santa Elena Canyon is a far cry from the tower skyscrapers of the big city. And it's a far-flung adventure just getting there. But it's an adventure that is worth every moment of the trip.

A GIN RESTORED

Burton

or more than one hundred years, cotton was the major crop in Texas. It sustained entire towns; it made folks rich. Great engines of the cotton gins throbbed from dawn until long past dark, and the air was rich with the smell of cottonseed. Then things changed, and cotton wasn't king anymore. Like a lot of other cotton towns of the past, Burton, Texas, appeared to be losing the battle against time and change. If it were not for one old relic left standing just off of Main Street, this tiny town might have disappeared altogether. But the Burton Farmers Cotton Gin has kept hope alive.

Doug Hutchison was a tourist who couldn't resist stopping in the small town with the same name as his hometown in Ohio. What he stumbled upon by accident one afternoon changed his life and the lives of the 300 residents of Burton.

Doug: *I was taking pictures of all the old historic things in town, and, half-jokingly I think, someone said, "You got to go over and see the old cotton gin." I took them serious. The back doors of the engine room were open, and I came around the corner real quick and went to jump in the gin, and there was this engine. I could not believe there was this huge engine in there. And as I walked through the gin, it was like walking back in time. It was spooky. The wind would blow gently, the cobwebs move—you got a feeling that someone just blew a whistle and everybody left, and they were gonna be back any time.*

It was Doug who convinced the town of Burton that this gin was worth preserving and restoring.

Doug: *This represents one of our most significant historical resources. It's intact—it has all the records plus the machinery. It's one of the last remaining of its type in the state. And because Texas is so significant in cotton production, that translated to national importance. We're one of the last remaining gins of this era in the nation.*

So in 1986 Operation Restoration was formed to save the gin. The goal was to get the old gin running again. And in their determination they attracted attention from as far away as Washington, D.C. Larry Jones, from the Smithsonian Institution, was on site to see the gin for himself.

> **Larry:** *This was almost like a time warp, where you step back in time. You can walk through this gin, and you can see the evolution of cotton harvesting from handpicked cotton on through to machine-picked cotton. It's all right intact in this gin, all the records, from the minutes of the very first meeting when it was decided to organize this gin. It's just an absolute treasure, what they found there. With a lot of sweat equity put into the thing, it'll gin cotton again. This is their ultimate goal—to gin again with this. To gin for the festivals.*

The last time the gin worked was in 1974. And today, the folks of Burton hope this cranky old machine will breathe life back into an entire town.

> **Doug:** *This is history. This is Burton's gin that ran for decades, and we now have the gin back. This is history for Burton remade. We're saving this gin for future generations—to show them what went on in a community like this. The children need to know what their parents and grandparents and great-grandparents established here. It's not made the history books because it's small-town history.*

Gins like the one in Burton built communities in small towns all across America. That memory's all but gone. But a piece of it's been saved in Burton, Texas, and all because a tourist from Burton, Ohio, took a joke seriously.

"YOU GOT A FEELING THAT SOMEONE JUST BLEW A WHISTLE AND EVERYBODY LEFT, AND THEY WERE GONNA BE BACK ANY TIME."

SINCE OUR STORY . . .

The Burton Cotton Gin has now been restored to full operation and it is listed on the National Register of Historic Places. Since we first produced our story, the volunteers restoring the gin have received technical assistance from the Smithsonian Institution, the Texas Historical Commission, The National Trust for Historic Preservation, and several area universities. The Burton Cotton Gin is located at 307 Main Street in Burton, Texas. It is open for tours on Friday and Saturday from 10:00 A.M. to 4:00 P.M. and on Sunday from 1:00 to 4:00 P.M.

ABOUT THE AUTHOR

Bob Phillips is executive producer and host of the popular television series *Texas Country Reporter*, which airs in syndication in all Texas television markets. The program first went on the air in 1972, and it has been celebrating the people and places on the backroads of Texas ever since.

Phillips is a native of Dallas and graduated from Southern Methodist University. He lives in Highland Village, Texas, and is the author of three previous books: *Texas Country Reporter Cookbook* (1990), *52 Offbeat Texas Stops* (1993), and *52 More Offbeat Texas Stops* (1997).

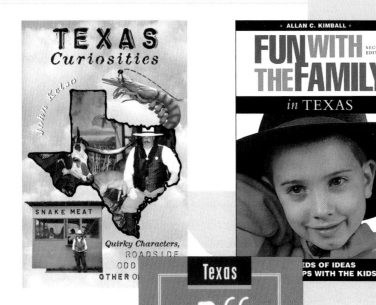

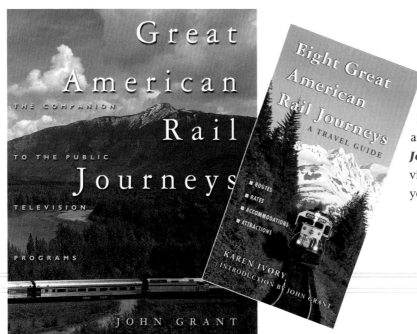